# PROPERTY MANAGEMENT EXCELLENCE

# PROPERTY MANAGEMENT EXCELLENCE

A VALUES-BASED APPROACH TO
REAL ESTATE AND PROPERTY INVESTING

ANTHONY A. LUNA

*Advantage* | Books

Copyright © 2025 by Anthony A. Luna.

All rights reserved. No part of this book may be used or reproduced in any manner whatsoever without prior written consent of the author, except as provided by the United States of America copyright law.

Published by Advantage Books, Charleston, South Carolina.
An imprint of Advantage Media.

ADVANTAGE is a registered trademark, and the Advantage colophon is a trademark of Advantage Media Group, Inc.

Printed in the United States of America.

10 9 8 7 6 5 4 3 2 1

ISBN: 979-8-89188-046-7 (Hardcover)
ISBN: 979-8-89188-047-4 (eBook)

Library of Congress Control Number: 2025900041

Cover design by Matthew Morse.
Layout design by Ruthie Wood.

This publication is designed to provide accurate and authoritative information in regard to the subject matter covered. It is sold with the understanding that the publisher is not engaged in rendering legal, accounting, or other professional services. If legal advice or other expert assistance is required, the services of a competent professional person should be sought.

> Advantage Books is an imprint of Advantage Media Group. Advantage Media helps busy entrepreneurs, CEOs, and leaders write and publish a book to grow their business and become the authority in their field. Advantage authors comprise an exclusive community of industry professionals, idea-makers, and thought leaders. For more information go to **advantagemedia.com**.

*To my wife, Lauren —*

*Your constant faith in me has been the steady beat behind every chapter of our wild adventure.*

*Through the late nights, the big risks, and all the uncertain roads, you never flinched—you just smiled and said, "let's go."*

*You're my partner in life, in business, and in every bold dream we dare to chase.*

*Thank you for standing by me, dreaming with me, and always letting your freak flag fly right alongside mine.*

*This book—and the life we're building together—is as much yours as it is mine.*

*Love you more than I can say with words,*

*Anthony A. Luna*

# CONTENTS

## PART I ..... 1
Learning Excellence from the Streets to the C-Suite

### INTRODUCTION ..... 3

### CHAPTER 1 ..... 7
Where the 110 Ends

### CHAPTER 2 ..... 19
A Mentor and a New Path

### CHAPTER 3 ..... 31
A Leap of Faith

## PART II ..... 47
The Principles

### CHAPTER 4 ..... 49
Listening and Communication

**CHAPTER 5** ............................................. **77**
Ethics and Integrity in All We Do

**CHAPTER 6** ............................................. **89**
Owner Mindset

**CHAPTER 7** ............................................ **107**
Quality of Life

**CHAPTER 8** ............................................ **137**
Building a Legacy

**CHAPTER 9** ............................................ **155**
Future Facing

**CONCLUSION** .......................................... **171**
Full Circle

**ABOUT THE AUTHOR** ................................... **175**

**CONNECT WITH ANTHONY A. LUNA** ....................... **177**

# PART I

# Learning Excellence from the Streets to the C-Suite

# INTRODUCTION

> *You cannot teach a man anything. You can only help him discover it within himself.*
> —GALILEO GALILEI

If you had told me when I was growing up as an at-risk kid in LA's Harbor Area that I would be the CEO of a property management company before the age of forty, I might have laughed at you (in fact, I definitely would have laughed at you). As a youth, I first had to even believe I could escape my circumstances, that I could see a life beyond gangs and drugs, a life where I could maybe help others.

Eventually, I dreamed of seeing myself as a leader—I wanted to make a difference in the lives of others like those who helped me see a future beyond my circumstances. I had once imagined myself leading a nonprofit like the Boys & Girls Clubs of the Los Angeles Harbor, but never in the world of for-profit business.

The story of how I became the CEO of Coastline Equity, a commercial and multifamily property management firm, has as much to do with values as it has to do with business—and it is the story I will share on these pages. Yes, I learned the business inside and out (and I love to problem solve!) from mentors and through experience, but it would all be meaningless if I was not living my purpose and beliefs. And those beliefs and principles, in turn, drive our reputation for property management excellence, and drive strong profits, because our values engender trust and loyalty. It all works together.

I never would have gotten to where I am today if my journey had been about myself alone. Instead, it has been about how my success can improve the lives of others and build stronger communities—because despite my background of poverty, I saw firsthand how the selflessness of a few could change the lives of many, and that inspired me to dream beyond my circumstances. No matter what is happening in the world around me, I am committed to making a difference through the work I do every single day. Every step of my journey has been fueled by the belief that we can create something greater together. I was mentored by people who shared that same vision. Now I want to share my commitment with you.

Along the way to my position at Coastline Equity, I like to think I learned from the people, obstacles, and triumphs along my journey—from mentors to people who were challenging to deal with, from the difficult circumstances of my childhood to the twists and turns no one, least of all me, could have predicted.

I now see the values I developed are part of the fabric of our company. Property management is a demanding business. It's not nine-to-five but is instead a twenty-four-seven business that requires nimble problem-solving, outside-the-box thinking, systems and processes that work, and the right tech—all of it—to achieve excellence. But excellence is not possible without that commitment to principles. Ours are:

# INTRODUCTION

- Listening and communication
- Ethics and integrity in all we do
- Owner mindset
- Quality of life
- Building a legacy

The principles are not just the bedrock of our company—they're the foundation of my life. My wife and I live this approach to excellence with compassion in everything we do because, at the end of the day, property management is not just about buildings and transactions; it is also about people. The tenants, the owners, our team, and the communities—we're all interconnected. Every decision we make impacts lives, and we never lose sight of the fact that behind every property is a person, business, or family relying on us.

I am a person of my word—or more than my word. Therefore, equality, responsiveness, and respect are at the heart of how we do commercial real estate and property management. Through my personal experiences as an at-risk youth living for most of my early life in Section 8 housing, I learned that everyone deserves a safe and comfortable place to live and work; everyone deserves their essential rights to be respected. We must approach the properties we own or manage, and the tenants we lease to, with curiosity, respect, and responsiveness. When we put these values front and center, we do our part in building communities where we can all be proud to work and live.

In addition, we manage properties for people for whom their real estate portfolio is their legacy—a long-term investment for the generations that follow. Our commitment to property management excellence ensures their properties maintain and grow in value, while we take the worry from them. And we believe that excellence isn't about status—it's about showing up every day and doing the right thing, even when it's hard, even when no one's watching.

I share my personal journey in this book because I think it demonstrates how these *Property Management Excellence* principles came to be the core of our business. But I also share because I think you can build wealth and success in your real estate portfolio without abandoning your principles—and your business and community will thrive because of it, not in spite of it.

If you're reading this, it's because you want to build something better. You want to grow your portfolio without compromising your values. You want to lead a team, not just manage a building. You want to do work that matters.

So let's get to work.

# CHAPTER 1

## Where the 110 Ends

> *The greater the obstacle, the more glory in overcoming it.*
> —MOLIÈRE

If you do not live in the Los Angeles area, you may not know that everything is divided by freeways and highways—and most of them are in gridlock constantly. It is not easy to get from point A to point B. But the neighborhood where I grew up in San Pedro is literally where the highway ends.

When I grew up—as well as most of my friends—we didn't leave San Pedro because there was really no way to get out of town. Los Angeles has a historically terrible public transportation system, and in many ways, we were cut off from the rest of the city. San Pedro was a blue-collar town in the 1990s and mid-2000s. There is a beach, but none of us went there as kids. At that time, it was not clean because it is part of the Los Angeles Harbor, the number-one port in the country and the number-two port in the world. Today, San Pedro remains a densely populated, working-class neighborhood undergoing a kind of renaissance and transformation of its own.

I had plenty of other strikes against me other than being from the "wrong side of town." I grew up in a single-parent household. My dad was a drug addict and a gang member and drifted in and out of my life. I always yearned for that interaction with him, but it never really happened—most of the time, there were many empty promises. My mom, in my early years, really tried to figure things out despite our circumstances—but it was not easy.

I remember the first home we lived in on Section 8 housing. A small white back house in San Pedro, tucked behind another, with an alleyway as our backyard. At night, the air was filled with the sharp pops of fireworks and the echo of gunshots, often indistinguishable from one another. As a kid, I never really knew which was which. I just knew to stay inside.

In the kitchen, my mom was working her magic. With food stamps stretched as far as they could go, she found a way to fill our home with warmth—making meals that honored her Italian roots and the Mexican recipes she had picked up from my dad's family. Simple dishes like fideo or homemade sugo over pasta became comfort food for me and my siblings—meals that said, We're okay, even when times were tough. That was her way of fighting for us, of anchoring us in love and heritage, even in the chaos.

There was a short period of time during which we were in a domestic violence shelter because my father was physically and verbally abusive. We ended up in that small white house thanks to the Section 8 program. It wasn't glamorous. But it was home. It was our normal. I saw the worst of the worst landlords while growing up in Section 8 housing, and some others who had compassion and tried to treat residents with decency. I experienced firsthand what treating

# CHAPTER 1

people with respect and dignity meant—and it informs my business to this day.

I never saw a particular career path when I was young—it was hard to even imagine getting past the end of the 110. In my elementary years, I can vividly remember thinking, "I don't want to go to jail; I don't want to go to prison." I had no visions of entrepreneurship or owning a company, just of wanting to avoid entering the justice system. That system seemed a rite of passage. Every man, in my child mind, *had* to go to jail or prison because every man I knew had been in jail or prison. The male figures in my friends' lives—*they* all had been in and out of prison. Every male figure who was in my life, including my dad—and by then, a stepdad, who at least improved our quality of life—was in and out of jail.

So how did I end up here? I am hoping that this book will educate people on property management and real estate investing—but I also hope it shows the immense power each of us holds to make a difference and create real change. Even in the toughest circumstances, we can nurture excellence and rise above. Around fifth grade, I had an incredible teacher who believed in me before I even believed in myself, and I could feel that. I can remember her telling my mother in a parent-teacher conference that "Anthony can go to college. It's something that he is capable of doing, and I can see him going to get an MBA and going to grad school."

I honestly don't think I really knew or fully understood what college was or realized that there was another option other than jail and prison. In fact, there were many options and a whole wide world beyond the end of the highway—I just didn't know how to reach them.

At the time, I was a member of the Boys & Girls Club. I had been a member my whole life, but I didn't become very active until this period. Then I started going every single day, starting in middle school through high school. I was there five days a week, and if they were open on the weekends, I was there too.

That's where all of my positive male role models came from. By now, as I mentioned, I had a stepdad. We went from being very poor to having a noticeable difference in our quality of life. For the first time, we had name-brand soda in the house and plenty of food, even toward the end of the month when finances used to be leaner. We went to Disneyland.

Things started to change, but not for the right reasons—he was a drug dealer. While I know he tried to take care of us, this was not the kind of role model I needed. Instead, the Boys & Girls Club provided tutors, then mentors, and then as I grew older, I worked there tutoring the younger kids and developing my leadership skills. The Club was the center of my world.

When high school came around—as it happens for many adolescents—my life got trickier. When I was younger, I was a top student, earned good grades, and was part of leadership programs, and even in high school, I was very active in the community, very active with the Boys & Girls Club. But in high school, I also developed a new love—I began DJing. I learned to DJ at the Boys & Girls Club and fell in love with hip-hop and fell in love with music. I think that love of music that speaks to us *also* is a hallmark of adolescence as we start to figure out who we are.

Lyrics mean so much to teens that we think our favorite rappers or singers are speaking directly to us and what we are going through. Hip-hop did that for me. However, these parties that I was throwing or DJing at did not always have the best environment. I didn't see it then, but I was heading down a dark part of my journey.

My mom would give me a hard time if I brought home a C—but there were all kinds of activities going on around me that could get me in much worse trouble. Every day, Monday through Thursday, I worked at the Boys & Girls Club as an employee, tutoring younger kids. I still loved the Club.

On the weekends, I worked at the fish market, and then when I was done at the fish market, I was out DJing. I was working a lot, and I was constantly distracted. I also think, in hindsight, I wasn't on anybody's radar, so to speak (I also now know I've been diagnosed with ADHD like so many entrepreneurs). I see now how that ability to do so many things and multitask is a superpower. But the rigid structure of school was also a problem for me—I struggled to focus.

I was surrounded by chaos at home and on the streets. But I was taking AP classes—because I *did* now understand that college might be a ticket for me out of the end of the 110. I was really pushing myself most of the time, but I'd frequently cut the classes that bored me. I was walking a very fine line—without much margin for error.

Meanwhile, Mike Lansing, the CEO of the Boys & Girls Club I attended, had a vision for a program that he wanted to develop called College Bound. At that time, fewer than 50 percent of kids who were going to my high school were graduating high school on time, let alone going off to college. Kids who were going to the Boys & Girls Club had even worse rates of graduation than that.

So he developed a program called College Bound based on this idea of, first, getting us to graduate high school, and second, getting us to understand that postsecondary education was attainable and teaching us how to get there, how to find financial aid, and how to apply for scholarships. I was in one of the first graduating classes of College Bound.

The program showed me in a more concrete way that college was attainable. I attended all the workshops and classes at the Boys & Girls Club that taught me how I could get there and which classes to take. The Club had to fill that role for me—because my school counselor did not believe I could go on academically and informed me I should just be OK with going to a trade school. I think the trades are wonderful—but I remember being really discouraged and going to the Club after school and saying that my school counselor had told me to give up my college dreams. Let me tell you, an amazing woman who had worked for the Boys & Girls Club for years blew a gasket. *She* made sure I took the classes I needed and that the colleges wanted to see on my transcript.

There were also two other people who were kind of the mom-and-dad figures of the teen center at the Boys & Girls Club. Hilda and Leo were the director and assistant director of the teen center. Leo was one of the people who taught me how to DJ, and Hilda ran all the leadership programs. I spent every day with them. Every weekend. They took us places and exposed us to new opportunities, and Leo began to mentor me in ways that showed me what it meant to be a man in society. It wasn't about the activities they could provide. It was about their *time,* the sense of belonging they nurtured and care they showed.

Before we as a society were ever talking about toxic masculinity, Leo was having those discussions in different ways, about how to treat a partner and how to go on a date and how to be respectful and how to iron your shirt and how to put deodorant on. So few people realize how much they learn by osmosis and being part of a world where those skills are a given.

To me and my friends at the Club, they weren't.

In San Pedro, there was a lot of gang activity, and my dad and my stepdad were affiliated with the Mexican gang in town—which at the time was having racial tensions with Black gangs. However, I grew up at the Boys & Girls Club, and at that time, most of the members were Black, and they were my friends. I tried to straddle two worlds. I

## CHAPTER 1

can recall seeing fights and people being stabbed, and I saw a drive-by near the Club.

But that Boys & Girls Club was our safe space, and they protected us. We knew how to get there fast. It wasn't far from our school—five blocks—but in that five-block span, shootings happened, stabbings happened. It was not a good time to be living in that area. We learned to move quickly and just get to the Club.

Finally, there was a big fork in the proverbial road of my future—and which way I would go was not a given. During my senior year in high school, I was applying to colleges. By this point, I knew I was going to college, but again, I was still living that fine line. I was DJing at big parties—and throwing them too. I was also sneaking into twenty-one-and-over clubs to DJ when I was way too young. I was doing my best to stay out of trouble—but I seemed to always find ways to put myself in environments where that could easily change.

Then there was a party that I got asked to DJ at in the fall of my senior year—and it was a party that was bound to have problems. It was being hosted at a house that was bound to have members of the Mexican gang attending. Meanwhile, I always attracted a Black crowd through my friends and classmates. Race relations in San Pedro were not good, and times were fraught in that regard.

Sure enough, a huge fight broke out, and several people pulled out guns and knives. Multiple friends were shot and stabbed—*and one of my good friends, L.T., was murdered that night.*

The police arrived, sirens and lights flaring, and I was suddenly a witness to my friend's murder. I understand needing to keep me there at the scene, but I was seventeen at the time—and I had watched my friend bleed out, completely traumatized and stuck at the scene, still staring at his lifeless body. I remember calling my mom, distraught, and telling her what happened.

As I was saying, in real emotional agony, "Someone from the Mexican gang killed L.T.," I heard my stepdad loudly in the background on the other end.

I could hear him saying, "Get off the phone. He needs to stop saying that out loud. Get him off the phone!" I was breaking a gangland code.

The next week was when I was supposed to pick the school where I was going to college. It should have been a time where I was looking forward to the future. However, in that same week, as I was trying to choose my future, I also had to go to L.T.'s funeral. It all blurred together. I was grieving, I was scared, I was angry—I was a mess of traumatic emotions.

So feeling like my home was no longer safe, knowing the streets where I was growing up were unsafe, and needing to get away and make a fresh start, I decided to go to Chico State, which was as close to the Oregon-California border as I had ever been—eight hours away.

*Far enough to get away from my past.*

Around this time, I met an unlikely man who would help me process everything I had been through. He took the anger I had over the murder of my friend—a murder still unsolved to this day—and really took what could have been fuel to keep fighting, a fuel to keep finding trouble, and instead channeled that in a way for me to focus it into a positive. And this was a local police officer.

In San Pedro, there was a local cop, Joe Buscaino, who was what is called a senior lead officer (he later served on the city council). He was the type of police officer in the LAPD who had boots on the ground in the community, was doing community building, and had a pulse on what was happening in town. He was a cop who often came to the Boys & Girls Club, and I had met him before, but I didn't have a great relationship with him and kept my distance from him.

# CHAPTER 1

Given my dad's and stepdad's backgrounds, police were not people I felt comfortable around.

After my friend's death, Joe approached me and said, "I'm starting to put this group together, and I've heard you're really angry with LAPD about what happened that night and how they addressed it."

This group (which Hilda encouraged me to join) was going to be a community advisory board for the police department. There was already an adult community police advisory board, called Community Police Advisory Board (CPAB), and it was all over LA for every division.

This was in the mid-2000s, and Joe wanted teens in the community to have a voice. Tensions with the police ran high. I was not sure at all that I wanted to be involved—and I explained specifically why. I told him I had been kept at the house where my friend was killed, and I wasn't allowed to leave, and they also did not cover the body.

Joe very empathetically explained why and how the incident was handled that way from the law enforcement perspective. Our deep conversation did not change the fact that it was a horrible event, and it wasn't going to bring L.T. back, but it did help me to see that there was more to the investigation than I understood at the surface. Speaking with him helped me logically understand things. Then he said, "Can you imagine if you actually got to help the department fix some of those things that you experienced?"

I thought about it and said yes. This is an approach I still believe in—being part of the solution rather than only complaining about the problem. I started participating and helped Joe not only launch teen CPAB in San Pedro in the harbor division but also actually spread across the entire LAPD, and by the time we were done, the idea was spreading elsewhere too. After graduation, I traveled with Joe to Atlanta to go speak at a conference about teen CPAB and how it was helping transform Los Angeles and helping keep teens engaged in a positive way with the police. Joe became a pivotal mentor in a really tough time for me.

He would bring me and some of the other teens on teen CPAB to city council meetings and say, "By the way, you have five minutes on the docket—I'm not speaking … you are." Here was someone teaching me more leadership lessons and skills. To this day, public speaking is not difficult for me.

When it was time for me to leave for college orientation, Joe asked if my mom was dropping me off. I explained that was not possible and that I would be taking buses—it would take me probably a dozen hours to get there, with transfers and stops. Joe really felt he or someone should drop me off and get me settled, but I was used to figuring things out on my own.

To me, though, that concern was such a powerful act of compassion.

However, despite being hours and hundreds of miles from the streets of San Pedro, the trauma stayed with me. It took a while for me to get used to this little rural college community, and for many months afterward, I was unhappy there. I still had all the fear and had night tremors from the whole experience of that horrible night and other experiences from my childhood and teenage years. I was always looking over my shoulder and always feeling like something bad was going to happen. It took really close college friends and fraternity brothers telling me, "You're fine here. You don't have to always be on guard. You don't have to always look over your shoulder."

I could not know it then, but these experiences—all of them, good and bad—were already shaping who I was going to be as a business owner (eventually) and community leader. My experience with housing insecurity and the sanctuary I found at the Boys & Girls Club helped me understand that everyone deserves a safe and comfortable place to live, work, and grow.

# CHAPTER 1

Although I didn't know back then that someday I would be managing living- and working-spaces for others, my experiences as a child and teen shaped my values. People like Hilda, Leo, and Joe were people who embodied integrity in all they did. That was something I was learning to carry forward in my own life.

When you deal with uncertainty as a child, it lingers in your DNA. So much of building a life of promise and not the streets was learning to trust. The people I found at the Boys & Girls Club were people who "showed up," in today's parlance. People like Joe treated me as a person deserving of respect and not just some "troubled teen" in the wrong place at the wrong time.

I finally understood, through my experiences, that I was being "heard" and seen—I felt *listened* to (another value I believe in). I felt supported and had a great deal of trust with my mentors at the Boys & Girls Club. However, in one of the stranger twists in my story, a mentor who at first seemed to have nothing in common with me ended up being the most profound influence on my life's work.

# CHAPTER 2

## A Mentor and a New Path

> *I don't care what you do for a living. If you do it well, I'm sure there was someone cheering you on or showing the way. A mentor.*
> —DENZEL WASHINGTON

Sometimes, a single moment can change the entire trajectory of our lives. Like a pebble dropped into still water, one encounter, one decision, can send ripples that shape our future in ways we never expect. Whether it's a mentor who sees potential we can't yet grasp or a simple act of compassion that shifts our perspective, these moments have the power to alter our path. It's only later that we can trace those ripples back and recognize how "fate" had a hand in guiding us.

When I was at the Boys & Girls Club, aside from Hilda and Leo, some of the kids were assigned mentors from the community. Originally, I was supposed to be partnered with a guy in the mortgage business. But when the housing market crashed, he went out of business and essentially disappeared from the Club. My best friend,

Adell, was matched with George Mayer, a businessman from the area. When George heard that my intended mentor had backed out, he ended up agreeing to take both Adell and me on together.

This was around 2006. George had started volunteering at the Club around two years before. After a family member by marriage passed away, George had learned that this gentleman had been very involved in the Boys & Girls Club in New York. With that inspiration and a desire to give back, George had not realized that he lived less than fifteen minutes from the Boys & Girls Club. He resided in Palos Verdes, which is an affluent part of the South Bay.

He did not know that less than five minutes from his home, there was an essential Boys & Girls Club with kids (like me!) who needed mentors and people to care about them. George went down to the Club and asked if he could be a volunteer and mentor. That Boys & Girls Club did not have a formal mentorship program at the time. When George realized there were so many kids who wanted and needed a mentor, he felt led to start a program. At that time, he was in his later sixties—with the energy of someone twenty years younger, always dressed in a very classy way, always sharp.

However, I was a "kid." I remember thinking, "What could this old man possibly know about my experiences, about what I am dealing with, about Adell's experiences?"

I received a powerful lesson regarding assumptions and judging a book by its cover when I discovered that George Mayer was a child survivor of the Holocaust. One of the first times I spent time with George, he took Adell and me to the Museum of Tolerance in Los Angeles, which is the educational arm of the Simon Wiesenthal Center, an internationally renowned Jewish human rights organization.

The Museum of Tolerance is dedicated to challenging visitors to understand the Holocaust in both historic and contemporary contexts and confronting all forms of prejudice and discrimination in our world today. The exhibits made the things Adell and I learned in social studies and history class come to life and provided us with real context, and we were there with someone who experienced it themselves. Seeing frayed striped prisoners' uniforms and black-and-white photos of kids our age, emaciated, along with children, old people, men, and women was powerful and moved us both.

On the drive home from the museum, I thought, "This man has experienced more than we ever can imagine."

Despite the horrors of his childhood, George did not have a trace of bitterness, which was another powerful lesson. He also took Adell and me to many of the things he enjoyed doing. He brought us along with him, exposing us to new experiences. We went to USC games, and we went to museums and plays; every time we met with him, we would go on a field trip of sorts. These adventures almost always ended up with us visiting LA restaurants to cap off our days together.

These were not super expensive or exclusive places, but they were the typical restaurants kids are often exposed to in Los Angeles. Since Adell and I rarely left San Pedro, it was all new to us. Like Hilda and Leo, George was showing us a world of possibilities—as well as teaching us how to operate in that world. How to belong there.

George was another exceptional person with compassion who showed up during some of my darkest moments. When L.T. died, he reached out, and I sensed that he was very invested in my staying safe and getting out of the community where I might be targeted or experience more violence around me. During the years when I left the area and attended college far away in Chico, George would check in with me—and he kept in touch with Adell too.

George also talked to Adell and me frankly and openly about how we were feeling and spoke to us about our emotions and made sure that we had that sounding board all this time. This was another important lesson he imparted to us. He was an example, not just of a successful man but also of one who was comfortable discussing feelings in a healthy way.

I had no idea what George did for a living (something you will likely find humorous at the end of the chapter). I knew he was in business and owned businesses and that he was very successful. He dressed like a successful person (and taught Adell and me how to tie our neckties). In my adolescent mind, George was just this amazing man in the community who had decided to give of his time to the Boys & Girls Club as a volunteer—albeit a volunteer with some extraordinary experiences that made him who he was.

Meanwhile, off in Chico, I changed my major a couple of times in college. I entered school planning on obtaining a music industry degree, then I switched into the business program. While attending a lecture on finance, the professor lectured that business and capitalism were about making as much money as possible at any cost. It didn't matter whom you tore down or whom you stepped on; it didn't matter how you treated others as long as you were profitable.

I was so turned off and disgusted by that way of thinking that the next week, I changed my degree for the third time. I decided from that experience that I was meant to work in the realm of nonprofits. To me, that made so much sense, as if it was what I was meant to do all along. I was working at the Boys & Girls Club in Chico and really enjoying what I was doing, so I decided to go into public administration.

However, I was also really struggling in college. In high school, I had been able to "skate" a little by virtue of being smart and showing up to most classes and acing the tests, even if I didn't always turn in my homework or pay close attention. But in college, the demands were heavier. I couldn't just show up without studying and get a good test score.

I also did not have my usual support system. I had gone from this amazing support system at the Boys & Girls Club that was always there to needing to figure things out on my own. I could walk into the Club, and if I had a problem, Leo would talk me through it, or if I needed to understand how to navigate taking the SATs, there was someone to show me. For anything, from academic issues to personal ones, I had this "family" at the Club. While I was used to being a kid who tried to solve his own problems and I was very independent, it did not mean that unease and loneliness did not permeate my college years.

I was alone in Chico, and my experiences left me feeling isolated. I only visited home twice the entire time I was in college. Around me, my fellow students would talk about going home for Thanksgiving or Christmas and the feasting they would be doing, about their grandmas cooking all kinds of dishes and moms doing their laundry for them because they were just happy they were home (at least for the first day or two), and about maybe even a ski trip or vacation someplace exotic and visits with high school friends. When summer rolled around, it was the same—all the plans, all the hometown love.

In my junior year, my mother moved up to Chico with my younger sister. My mom was struggling in her own way. She had been a teenage mom when she had me, so she was not well equipped to parent—she was still growing up herself. My stepdad (the drug dealer) was financially supporting all of us, and when he finally got deported and lost his green card, she could not make it work on her own.

Here I was, a broke college student living on ramen and peanut butter sandwiches, and there were a few times when I was sending money home. I knew just enough about personal finances to know that this just did not make sense. I was sending money from Chico to LA, and the cost of living was so much more there.

I suggested to my mother that she and my younger sister move to Chico. I would rent a larger apartment, and the three of us would live together and split the costs. This was, without a doubt, a terrible decision. It was a positive for my sister, but it was terrible for me. And it was not good for my mom.

In the pain of loss, my stepfather going away, and her difficult financial predicament, and with few healthy coping skills, my mom began drinking heavily and relying on me to watch over my sister. Our mom was unreliable, at times not showing up when we needed her to since the three of us shared a car. The added responsibilities and stress of my family situation, on top of the fact that I was already struggling in school, were enough to derail my education. I dropped out after my junior year.

I was ready to return to San Pedro—and the Boys & Girls Club. It was a calling as much as a job. The best part about it was working with the kids. That was my gift, I believed. I also knew that the kids were aware of my story—perhaps some of them could see themselves following a path to college or a path that was off the streets, not headed to jail. I was just like them—same streets, same sorts of circumstances.

I had been managing the teen center in Chico. In fact, I wasn't quite twenty-one, and that was typically frowned upon, but in my case, I had a relatability that allowed me to connect with the kids. Now I would be returning to the Club of my own childhood. It felt like a full-circle moment.

It was in my twenties, feeling fulfilled, that I had found a place and a career where I belonged and could bloom. About this time, I met my wife, Lauren, at the Boys & Girls Club where she was also working as an aspiring social worker. We shared the same passions for helping kids, for helping the community, and for giving back. (And later we discovered a shared passion for travel.)

She was (and is) my best friend, and before too long, we were making plans to get married. I thought I was going to stay in the nonprofit world forever. I had this dream of becoming the CEO of the Boys & Girls Club I grew up in. The people around me saw that potential in me, and I felt like I was racing up the corporate ladder within the nonprofit world.

It was all a rosy picture.

In the meantime, I was also a pragmatist. No one goes into the world of nonprofit work (or at least they shouldn't) expecting to get rich. I began moonlighting in the property management world as a side gig. I knew, even with earning promotions and ascending the nonprofit ladder, it would be a while before I could fully be comfortable on my salary—particularly if Lauren and I were to be married and start a family.

At this point, Lauren had decided to return to school for a graduate degree in social work. The program was accelerated, and students could not work full time while pursuing it. This was another motivation for my decision to enter property management. By now we were living together and planning for our wedding—and we were minus one full-time salary while she was back in college. Lauren and I thought she could at least do some office functions, etc., and help out part time if we got some properties to manage.

Property management was something I could do to supplement my income—with Lauren as my partner in that—and augment my salary. In what certainly sounds like an unusual opportunity, I was looking on Craigslist for potential positions, and I found an investor who was seeking someone to manage his real estate portfolio. Craigslist is an odd place to advertise for a portfolio manager, but I reached out.

This was an "on-site" property manager role, something that is very common in our area. In fact, in the state of California, if there are more than sixteen units, an on-site manager is required. But this was not solely an on-site manager job. This gentleman was basically seeking someone interested in essentially starting their own business to then exclusively work on his portfolio, which had over 250 units, primarily in Long Beach.

I sent an email detailing my interest, and he emailed me back forms and an online assessment in order to apply. Then he agreed to meet with me. He was pretty frank that since I did not have experience, he had not planned on even interviewing me. However, when I took the automated assessment test (after other applicants scored abysmally), my score was so high, he felt he would at least speak with me.

He listened as I explained my interest. I had grown up in all sorts of apartments and felt I had insights—and my nature of multitasking and wanting each day to be a challenge and different certainly suited property management. It is most definitely not a nine-to-five job, and you are often putting out proverbial fires.

He asked if I would be managing the properties myself or with someone. I mentioned Lauren. He suggested that she take the same assessment—and if she did well, the three of us would meet and discuss potential next steps. Lauren scored just as well as I did on this assessment.

We scheduled a coffee meeting, and he was honest: "I don't know why I'm meeting you guys when I have more qualified candidates. Anthony, you scored really high. Normally, the partner is a completely different personality. So they often score really poorly. Lauren, you support basically the same strengths as Anthony.

"So I felt I had to meet with you two."

He showed us the portfolio of properties he owned. He had started his career in the hospitality industry and had been an executive for the Marriott Hotel brand. I think he was willing to take a chance on us, as he enjoyed training people for Marriott. So once again in a fateful way, this was the perfect opportunity and fit.

He got to mold Lauren and me into his vision of how he wanted his portfolio managed, and we made a huge leap into a large portfolio as newbies in the industry and learned all we could about what was involved in property management while gaining real experience. Not only that, but he was also generous with his knowledge. Since we were new to the business, we had many questions—and he was terrific about answering them and was a wealth of wisdom.

At the time, I was doing both jobs—working as a director at the Boys & Girls Club and running this real estate company's portfolio. When I first returned to San Pedro, I was the director of high school services—a position that was a dream job for me (except perhaps the pay). I was working around the kids, which had always been my passion. I was working twelve- to-sixteen-hour days, and I loved it. I worked at the Boys & Girls Club on paperwork and programming until the kids came for after-school time. Then I would facilitate programs with the kids and stay busy that way until late in the evening.

However, soon I was promoted to a desk job. I felt like I was merely clocking in and clocking out. Yes, I could produce reports and hire the right people, and the Club was running smoothly, but most of the time, I was miserable behind a desk and in meetings.

This was therefore the impetus to give property management a real try. I felt like I had the bandwidth to take on this portfolio. In addition, I had enough business knowledge now to understand that real estate is often a path to financial freedom. I wanted that freedom, a better quality of life for myself and for Lauren and any future family we had. I also had visions of philanthropy—being able to give back. Real estate was my path.

As a kid from a low-income community, from a poor family, I had a barrier of entry to enter into real estate. I did not have the capital. I did not have a parent or grandparent who was going to help me put a down payment on a house. I couldn't move home to save money for that future purchase. If I was going to get a stronger foothold in the dream of a better life, this was a possible map.

As Lauren and I started managing the properties, there was definitely a learning curve. In fact, the learning went two ways. We were discovering and absorbing new things daily, and Robert, the man who owned the properties, was learning from us.

For years, he had a property manager who was amazing and "old school." Like the great managers of the seventies, eighties, nineties, or early two thousands, she could walk on a property and know all the names of the paint colors—all in her head. Later I worked with a similar manager at Coastline Equity—she could rattle off the scientific names of every tree or plant on the property, when they bloomed, and when they needed to be pruned. But it was all informal knowledge—old-fashioned paper knowledge—and when they left or retired, all of it went with them.

Now here Lauren and I were—two millennials. We were excited about all the ways we could leverage technology, create standard operating procedures and best practices, and manage the portfolio with new energy.

Robert had just purchased the software—the latest and greatest at the time. He was trying to learn it, but for Lauren and me, digital natives, we were completely comfortable with the program in a couple of days. (I was already familiar with it because the apartment complex where I lived was already using it.)

# CHAPTER 2

Although I was a Boys & Girls Club kid without the advantages of computers and fancy tech at home, our Club had an incredible CEO. He was a fundraising machine, very inspirational, and had incredible ideas. He had computer labs built at our Club in the 1990s. But this was not all about fun and games. In order to encourage us to learn how to use a computer and access the internet, in order to get computer game time for an hour, we had to complete lessons on using the computer or scavenger hunts online to learn new skills and learn how to research.

As technology evolved, so did the equipment and tech that the Club CEO purchased and had installed. He built a STEM lab. I actually had great exposure to technology at a young age—and this comfort with tech continues today.

Soon Robert was enjoying the financial freedom of being a real estate owner with his portfolio in capable hands. And by "soon," I mean about two weeks after we started. He said, "This was poorly planned, but I'm actually leaving for the Philippines for the next three weeks or so. We are going to have some communication issues with the time difference and everything else. I trust you, guys; you got this."

He had taken us to the bank to show us how to deposit 250 rent checks. We had the software. We were cramming our brains with as many facts about the properties as possible. It was very much sink or swim—and we were left on our own so quickly.

*And we swam.*

Robert also introduced us to real estate investing, and it was through him that I began to grasp what property management excellence was and what vision was at the heart of it. Robert was purchasing neglected historical buildings in downtown Long Beach—properties with vintage charm that had fallen into disrepair. His background in hospitality gave him the unique ability to see beyond the decay, to envision what these buildings could become with the right care and transformation.

I found myself deeply connecting to this process. It reminded me of mentoring a kid who, like me, was a little rough around the edges but had untapped potential. There was something thrilling about turning a neglected property into something beautiful and valuable—something you'd be proud to hand over, and that an owner would be proud to call their own. This style of real estate investing sparked a new passion in me: the art of transforming the forgotten and ignored into something exceptional.

I was also learning the principles that would form the bedrock of my approach to property management, things like listening to your properties. I watched Robert listen to the faint whisper of what a building could be. But I also learned, which I discuss in Part II, that listening to your buildings can alert you to problems before they become crises.

I was thriving in my new career. I had met my now-wife. I was back "home" in the community I cared about. Meanwhile, I had seen my old mentor, George, at community events and Boys & Girls Club fundraisers—always a pleasure.

After I had been working with Robert for a while, I attended a dinner being held for my friend Adell, and George was there. It was a social setting where we could really talk about life a little bit and not just the Boys & Girls Club budget and programming.

He asked me what I was doing. I explained my new career.

And then George marveled. "You don't know what I do after all this time, do you?"

I didn't.

It turns out that George was in property management. *And my life was about to have another twist.*

# CHAPTER 3

## A Leap of Faith

*I have learned that success is to be measured not so much by the position that one has reached in life as by the obstacles which he has had to overcome while trying to succeed.*
—BOOKER T. WASHINGTON

A few weeks after I reconnected with George at the dinner, we got together for lunch. As I sat across from him, it felt almost surreal—as if fate, or perhaps something greater, had brought me back to the man who had shaped so much of my early life. The same man who had mentored me as a teenager was now offering me a place in his world. I had somehow landed in the very profession he had mastered, and here I was, at twenty-seven years old, discussing the possibility of becoming a junior partner at Coastline Equity someday. It was one of those rare moments where everything feels like it's clicking into place, and I couldn't help but marvel at the unexpected turns life had taken.

George was in his late seventies by then, but he was as sharp and driven as ever—one of those people who seemed to defy time. His mind was always racing ahead, laying the groundwork for Coastline Equity's future. He spoke about a succession plan, about building something that would outlast both of us. When I decided to join him as a partner, the plan was for him to stay deeply involved until he was ready to retire, but I quickly realized that retirement wasn't in George's vocabulary. He thrived on the challenges, just as I did. Walking away from the business didn't sit well with either of us—there was still too much to build, too many problems to solve. We were just getting started.

Coastline Equity was also in need of a tech overhaul. The property management industry was ripe for innovation, and I was eager to bring my expertise to help Coastline Equity scale its third-party management services and streamline its processes. I had already been working with AppFolio, the most cutting-edge proptech ("property technology") software at the time, which I knew could revolutionize how we operated—if implemented correctly.

George had purchased the same software about eight months earlier, but the rollout had been rocky. He hadn't sunsetted his previous software system, because the numbers weren't adding up, and the system was plagued with glitches that needed fixing. My joining Coastline Equity started out as something of an experiment—George wanted to see what I could bring to the firm, and I was testing the waters too. I wasn't quite sure that I was ready to make such a big move myself. He had been a mentor to me, but working together was a different dynamic entirely. We both knew that success here wasn't just about business—it was about protecting the relationship we had built.

In my first weeks, I stared at spreadsheets, dug into the tech, and rooted out what was working and what wasn't in the software, and then trained the team to utilize the tech tools that would make their lives easier—and the company more efficient. From there, my role expanded quickly—and it was exciting for me to see the tangible difference I could make.

At the time, Coastline Equity had just six or so employees (as of this writing, we have over fifty). Originally, I functioned as an operations manager, so my hands were in everything. This was basically the best, most comprehensive education into the property management industry that I could have received. I was tasked with managing the most problematic properties we had at that time. I interacted with the most difficult challenges and most difficult properties—properties that had construction issues or active renovations.

I was dealing with general contractors, inspecting properties, interacting with tenants and residents on a twenty-four-seven basis, and handling emergencies. I was also managing the accounting team and investigating and trying to discern why they were struggling with the software. I was talking with clients, and I was also doing business development. I was doing a little bit of everything. As I wrote earlier, property management is not for those who want a nine-to-five job. It is unpredictable, exhilarating, exhausting, and fulfilling all at the same time.

While I had learned so much from my first position in property management, now, doing this full-time with George, I was seeing every aspect—and learning from someone who embodied the values I knew were essential to success.

At my first property management job with Robert Thomas, Lauren and I had engaged in conversations with him about equity in housing, the health of the community, and the importance of addressing the housing crisis—not only in San Pedro but also in communities across all of the United States. George also was concerned about equity, philanthropy, and helping the community. Along with core values that aligned with my own personal ones, I was learning the essentials to property management excellence.

Meanwhile, about two and a half years after I joined Coastline Equity, by now a partner, along came a shock to the world as a whole—the COVID-19 pandemic. The ravages of the pandemic impacted every business—including, obviously, property management. Rents in many areas were halted, impacting our clients and investors. People were staying home (more wear and tear in apartments and nearly no traffic at our commercial properties), and getting work or repairs done while trying to practice social distancing created new problems. In addition, Los Angeles had some of the strictest quarantine rules in the country, so people *literally* had to be off the streets—and that impacted our team as they, too, had to work from home.

Fortunately for us, our technical acumen and early adoption to proptech meant we could make some of the transitions with more ease than other companies in our sector. But of course, the biggest issues of the pandemic were the emotional and mental health tolls this global pandemic was taking on our loved ones and the communities around us. Children were kept at home, losing out on socialization. Parents were stretched to their limits. Meanwhile, cable news and our social media feeds were reminding us how very deadly this virus was.

Nowhere was this more apparent, beyond being a partner at Coastline Equity, than in my own family.

For my wife, Lauren, and social workers and teachers, healthcare professionals, and frontline essential workers, the pandemic was particularly brutal. Impacting Lauren, as a school social worker (she had by now completed her degree), were decisions being made at the superintendent level to ensure there was a social worker in every school in the LA Unified School District. Thus, Lauren went from

# CHAPTER 3

being at one school to being at three schools, and the caseload was just unmanageable. It was simply unrealistic, and she was starting to feel like she couldn't truly impact the lives of such a large caseload.

Consequently, she felt incredibly conflicted. She was the person the kids were relying on—but if there was a crisis at one school and she was assigned to a different school that day, she was not able to go to the one in crisis to help those students. Sometimes, career choices are made for you—when you can no longer live with the policies and choices being dictated. I had left the Boys & Girls Club when I was no longer directly serving young people. In Lauren's case, the situation in the school system was untenable.

Lauren, all this time, had been helping in the business during summer and winter breaks. With the situation in the schools unworkable, I asked her to come aboard at Coastline Equity full time. By now we had grown, so our first order of business was to create a human resources department—a new one. This was a perfect fit for Lauren, who has deep compassion and understanding of people.

I had read and then shared with her a book called *The Dream Manager*, by Matthew Kelly. The central concept is a question: What if you work for a company, the goal of which is to make your dream—your personal dream, that is—come true? Wouldn't you want to work for that company as long as you live?[1]

We were excited to have a concept of an HR team that not only focuses on our team members but also focuses on their full well-being and their aspirations. How did we help them fulfill their own dreams—while helping our team build ours?

Then, around 2022, Lauren and I started to talk about the possibility of buying the remainder of George's shares in the company. It was five years into the partnership between George and me, and

---

1   Matthew Kelly, *The Dream Manager* (Hyperion, 2007).

## PROPERTY MANAGEMENT EXCELLENCE

Coastline Equity had grown and prospered. However, I was now in my early thirties with a few years of property management (and plenty of trials by fire) under my belt. I had ideas about ways we could grow and evolve. By this point, though, George was in his eighties—still sharp and still with all that accumulated knowledge of property management. However, having two partners separated by over five decades showcased a couple of the ways we were different.

Our values, along with commitment to business practices like ethics, integrity, fairness, and equality, remained the same. But like most people contemplating retirement, he was looking to derisk his life, his workload, and his portfolio. He wanted to slow down, and I don't think he was interested in trying to fast-track growth at that point in Coastline Equity's history and where he was in his own life. He also still had plenty to keep him busy and passionate—serving on local nonprofit boards and being heavily involved at his temple.

At the same time, my mind was constantly racing with ideas to streamline operations, integrate new technology, and explore new investment opportunities. I was comfortable with taking on more risk and eager to expand quickly—but smartly. However, when it came to risk and growth, George and I often found ourselves at odds. While I was pulling together the threads of bigger, bolder deals—knowing that larger ventures come with greater risk—George was more cautious, often hesitant to dive into these high-stakes opportunities. And I completely understood where he was coming from.

There was a great deal to consider and weigh regarding this decision. First, I had to be sure my relationship with George would be preserved. And it has been.

Next, despite wanting to take Coastline Equity to new heights, this was to be a huge personal risk. Lauren and I would be assuming this financial and personal risk together. We would be business owners and entrepreneurs. Soar or crash—it would be completely on us.

The idea that we would become successful business owners in our early thirties was definitely exciting—and unsettling. It was a dream—and also scary. I could not look to my parents, or those in the community where I grew up, and see a model for this path. We didn't have a nest egg or safety net to fall back on if we failed.

*This was our leap of faith.*

In addition, it was a change from the path that I thought I was destined for my whole career. I had been in the for-profit world for a few years by then, but this would mean committing on a whole other level. Over time, I realized that I was remarkably suited to this new career of mine. I also realized, in terms of sheer impact, I could have more impact on the community by sitting on the board of the Boys & Girls Club or, as I will discuss later, through building and managing more affordable housing that was well run and well built and would make a difference to vulnerable populations and the community as a whole.

After sleepless nights, lots of long talks, and financial calculations, at the end of 2022, Lauren and I bought the remainder of George's shares that were outstanding. We were the sole owners of Coastline Equity. We had the freedom to implement our ideas for growth and innovation. We wanted to embrace the changes we felt would make us better—while maintaining the core values and principles that had sustained Coastline Equity since George Mayer founded it in 1972.

Coastline Equity initially existed to manage George's personal portfolio, as well as those of friends, family, and a few clients. However, from when I first joined as partner, to the end of our second year as sole owners, we grew three times over. Our predictions for the next few years are exponential.

I definitely have an innate drive and ambition and a growth mindset, but I think the experience I have gained from an organization called the Entrepreneurs' Organization (EO) has been invaluable in this expansion. Often, as entrepreneurs, we are operating alone or with a small team. In fact, I feel lucky that I can bounce things off Lauren when I have an idea or a problem. Still, part of the EO's benefit to me has been in having conversations with peers, talking about what's working in the business and what's not, and having experienced people share their own entrepreneurial struggles, the challenges and realities. Generally, other entrepreneurs share a similar mindset.

Driving growth, by the way, is not limited to the private sector. When I was with the Boys & Girls Club, the questions top of mind were often: What is the largest number of children we can serve? What's the biggest impact we can make? How can we be the best at what we do? I don't think, for me as a leader, it has ever been about what type of business or nonprofit I am working in. Instead, it has always been about having that growth mindset and always wanting to do more and serve more and be of service, whether it's serving clients and tenants or serving young people at a Boys & Girls Club.

Fortunately, Coastline Equity had always been a place of property management excellence, so when it came time to transition to Lauren's and my leadership, it frankly went more smoothly than I had even hoped—our existing clients were very happy with us. In fact, I personally called all of our key clients as that transition was happening just to let them know they were going to receive an email from George to explain what was occurring and that the process should be seamless, but that I wanted to call them first.

I remember one of our longest-standing clients, who had been with Coastline Equity for over thirty-five years. When I explained the reason for the call, he casually responded, "How is that different from the last couple of years? I thought George was already retired and was just consulting." It was a moment of relief for me, realizing that the trust George and I had built over the years had paid off. Our clients already felt secure, knowing their investments were in capable hands.

That trust is something we've earned through consistent dedication and an approach that goes beyond the basics. In Part II of this book, I'll outline the key principles we use to deliver superior service, but here's a preview of what we do to build and maintain that trust:

- **Clear, detailed financial reporting.** We provide itemized monthly reports that break down every expense and include supporting documentation, receipts, and descriptions. Our clients know exactly where their money is going, which builds trust and ensures financial transparency.

- **Maintenance transparency through documentation.** For every maintenance request, we provide "before and after" photos and detailed reports to both owners and tenants. This level of accountability reassures clients that issues are being addressed promptly and thoroughly, reinforcing their confidence in our services.

- **Simplified, transparent lease agreements.** We create easy-to-understand lease addenda that highlight critical terms such as rent escalation dates, maintenance responsibilities, insurance requirements, and payment options. This ensures that both tenants and owners are on the same page, reducing confusion and disputes.

- **Tailored services for each client.** We recognize that no two properties or investors are the same. We offer customized services to meet the unique needs of each client, ensuring that our approach aligns with their goals and long-term objectives.

- **Full-service property care and management.** From thorough property inspections to liability management, staff recruitment, and round-the-clock maintenance, we take a comprehensive approach to property management that covers all aspects of care.

- **Transparent vendor management.** For any expenses over $500, we provide three competitive bids and full transparency to ensure clients receive the best value for their investment.

It is also important to talk for a moment about commitment, not just to business but also to giving back. One of the things that always impressed me about George was his deep commitment to philanthropy. Over the years, I have met so many incredible people and organizations that dedicate their time and resources to support causes like the Boys & Girls Clubs, as well as other organizations.

George set a standard at Coastline by committing 2 percent of our top-line revenue to charitable donations. This wasn't just a token gesture; it was a meaningful contribution that reflected his values.

As Coastline grew, Lauren and I decided to take that commitment even further. We set a goal to donate 50 percent of our adjusted gross income—half of our profits—to causes we deeply care about. Yes, that's a significant shift, but it's directly tied to the company's performance. We believe that when the company thrives, our community should thrive alongside it.

We also extend that commitment to our team. If any team member donates to a charity, we'll match those contributions. This mindset fuels our entire team at Coastline Equity—it's embedded in our corporate culture. We're a goal-oriented group, and it's not just about hitting financial targets. We openly talk about the company's revenue goals and the impact those numbers will have on our charitable contributions. When we set ambitious goals, it might seem scary at first, but the excitement and purpose drive everyone forward. We know that every milestone we reach means more support for the causes we believe in, and that's something we're all proud to work toward.

We believe we have found the formula for *Property Management Excellence*, but calling it a "formula" makes it sound a little cold. The real secret is people. The lessons I learned from my childhood remain at the heart of everything we do. It's about more than just managing properties. We have a responsibility to care for our residents, tenants, and the communities we serve. Success in this business begins with compassion, and that's how we lead every day. The other side of the equation is we have an absolute fiduciary duty to do right for the other "people" in property management: our clients and investors. We approach every decision with an owner mindset—so that we absolutely safeguard their properties. For most of our clients, they're coming to us with their prized possessions, whether it is a monetary investment in a project or a property or portfolio itself. We have an unwavering responsibility to manage that property in such a way that we are thinking like the client; we are thinking like the owner; we are making those financial decisions or the strategic decisions with their interests in mind.

One of the most rewarding parts of our role is turning around properties that have been poorly managed. Frequently, clients inherit a portfolio of properties they don't have the time or desire to manage on their own, and it's often clear that the previous management company (or their parents) have let certain things go over time. Oftentimes we see where a previous management company has cut corners so much the property has lost value. A simple example might be instead of mitigating mold from a plumbing issue, the mold has simply been painted over, masking the problem.

In these cases, we balance being the financial stewards while ensuring the property is well cared for—which, in turn, cares for the tenants. Happy tenants are tenants that renew leases. When we can take a neglected property and make that inheritance a legacy property, it is very satisfying.

There's something very satisfying about solving a problem for someone. I can remember feeling pride at the Boys & Girls Club when kids arrived who were difficult, angry, or combative. Often, I could see a spark of leadership potential, even when they were channeling it in the wrong direction. When I could channel that spark into one of our leadership programs and watch that kid transition into someone who was leading in all the right ways, I would feel proud that we had a major impact on someone's life. I am sure that for Hilda, Leo, George, Mike, Joe, and others who saw something in me, it is a similar feeling.

That same compassion and energy for the "struggling ones" is probably why I like dealing with the most difficult properties. I find joy in tackling clients' financial or structural challenges. There's nothing quite like turning a struggling property into a class-A asset—it brings a sense of pride and accomplishment.

When we hire property managers, we make it clear: This career is about solving other people's problems, issues, and stress. If that doesn't energize you, then property management is not the right career for you.

I remember before Lauren joined the team full time, I would come home from work, and she would ask the age-old question, "How was your day?"

"It was a good day."

"What does that mean?"

"It was boring."

Now for many people, "boring" sounds like a lousy day. But in property management, a boring day is a good day. In fact, if you can get two or three of those boring days in a row, even better. Because I promise you, the next thing you know, there is a major storm coming in off the coast, and twenty-four hours of pounding rain will inevitably mean a drain system on at least one property will be problematic, and someone's roof is going to leak!

## Our Values

At the end of the day, I suppose it was the years I spent at the Boys & Girls Club that got me thinking about who I am and what my values are. I was fortunate enough to work with people in my career who taught me even more about how to manage properties with excellence and distinction.

Coastline Equity's core values are part of our DNA. Our three values are:

1. Equity for all

2. Growth mindset

3. Customer first (and the customer is all of our stakeholders)

Equity for all is the cornerstone of compassion—and recognizing that tenants from subsidized housing on up to the corner penthouse overlooking the ocean deserve equal respect in how they are treated.

A growth mindset is everything about how Coastline Equity is approaching the next five years, ten years—and beyond. I am excited, as the book progresses, to share some of the insights I've gained as far as how to protect and grow real estate investments.

Putting the customer first involves more than the investor or client. It includes doing right by all our internal and external stakeholders, from developing our team, to caring for tenants, to helping our vendors become knowledgeable on the unique insurance and other regulatory issues pertaining to property management so the vendors can grow along with us, to handling investors looking to entrust us with their assets. With strong leadership, compassion, knowledge, collaboration, and transparency, Coastline Equity really does lead the way by ensuring we put *all* our customers first.

Our core values help us build our core purpose:

*Leading with heart, empowering people, impacting communities.*

I know that does not sound like a "typical" purpose for a property management company. But then again, our commitment to people separates us from the rest, I think. In my opinion, if we embody that purpose, and we hold fast to our values—all the rest will fall into place.

Now I want to move on to the principles that we utilize to ensure we fulfill our mission to our clients, stakeholders, and communities. Each of the next chapters will explore one aspect:

### THE PRINCIPLES

**Listening and Communication**

You will learn that if you know how to "listen," your properties will tell you what they need. But listening and communication are also the bedrock of collaboration and community—and as an organization, we're learning the most efficient ways to ensure the team communicates with each other—and the people we serve.

### Ethics and Integrity in All We Do

We are often called in when a property has been mismanaged. Yes, we bring our knowledge and our forward-thinking approach, but our ethics and integrity are by far the reason we stand above the rest. It's hardwired into the company—since 1972!

### Owner Mindset

We take the growth of our clients' assets, our company's talent, and our company's reach seriously—we want to have the biggest impact we can.

### Quality of Life

We want our tenants to have safe and well-maintained residences, we want our commercial tenants to love their commercial space, and we want our clients to have worry-free asset management.

### Building a Legacy

Very often, real estate holdings are legacy properties for families to build a legacy and generational wealth—we take our duty of care very seriously to protect that legacy. Coastline Equity also wants to build our own legacy in impact on clients', tenants', team members,' and communities' lives.

## PROPERTY MANAGEMENT EXCELLENCE

I encourage you to scan the QR code below to learn more about Coastline Equity's mission. But now, let's move on to Part II, where we will learn the secrets of listening to your properties (and people!).

# PART II

# The Principles

# CHAPTER 4

## Listening and Communication

*Most of the successful people I've known are the ones who do more listening than talking.*
—BERNARD BARUCH

When I think about what mentors at the Boys & Girls Club provide, it is not just guidance. They are adults who listen—and for many adolescents and kids, that is what they need most. However, it is probably what every single one of us needs too. I think we all learned during the isolation of the COVID-19 pandemic that connection and communication are extremely important to our well-being.

Listening and communication are also part of the DNA of Coastline Equity. This encompasses listening to *all* our stakeholders from tenants to clients, as well as every single one of our team members, our vendors, and our larger community. We listen to our property owners. But it is also part of our philosophy to listen to our *properties*.

# Listening to Our Properties

Yes, as a people-centered company, we listen to our tenants, our people, our investors. But we also listen to our actual buildings—you would be surprised what they will tell you if you listen. Our concept of listening to our properties has several facets. First, it involves listening to our tenants. Residents and commercial tenants will tell you why they are attracted to a property. If they are dissatisfied, I promise they will also tell you why they are leaving. And if tenants start leaving—you've lost the battle.

Residential tenants do not want to move. Commercial clients prefer not to move. It is costly, stressful, and inconvenient, and it can result in loss of business, etc. So if someone waits to tell you they are leaving and the decision has already been made, then obviously, opportunities for communication were missed along the way.

There are a number of ways that we try to get feedback from the tenants. We put out a newsletter to our tenants, and in that newsletter there's always a way to leave a review and give us feedback—good or bad.

In addition, every time a tenant submits a work order, which is maintenance related, an automatic survey is sent to them through our proptech. Were they satisfied with the overall service? Was it completed fully? And do they have any other issues they want to report?

Then there's an annual tenant satisfaction survey that goes out to each and every tenant. As you can see, this is detailed around every area of tenant satisfaction. We can't improve if we don't know our issues. If you are a property manager, examine your tenant satisfaction survey (you should have one!) to ensure it asks the questions essential to your business.

# ESSENTIAL TENANT SATISFACTION SURVEY QUESTIONS

**Maintenance and Repairs:**

- Was your recent maintenance request handled within the promised time frame?
- How would you rate the quality of the repair work completed?
- Did the maintenance technician or vendor demonstrate professionalism and respect during their visit?

**Customer Service:**

- How satisfied are you with the overall level of customer service provided by the property management team?
- Were your concerns or questions addressed promptly and effectively?
- How would you rate the professionalism and communication skills of the property management staff?

**Building Condition and Amenities:**

- How satisfied are you with the cleanliness and upkeep of common areas (e.g., lobby, hallways, gym, etc.)?
- Are the property's amenities (e.g., laundry, parking, recreational areas) meeting your expectations?
- Are there any specific improvements you would like to see in the property's facilities?

**Communication and Responsiveness:**

- How would you rate the property management team's communication about important updates or issues (e.g., maintenance, renovations, policy changes)?
- How quickly are your questions or concerns typically addressed by the management team?
- Do you feel informed about upcoming events or building updates?

**Safety and Security:**

- How safe do you feel in your building and surrounding area?
- Are there any concerns related to security that we could improve?

**Sense of Community:**

- Do you feel a sense of community within the building or complex?
- What could be done to enhance the community experience for residents?

**Lease Renewal and Satisfaction:**

- How likely are you to renew your lease when it expires?
- What factors would influence your decision to renew or leave?

**Showing Experience:**

- On a scale of 1 to 10, how satisfied were you with the showing?
- What's one thing we could do to improve your showing experience?

**Overall Experience:**

- On a scale of 1 to 10, how satisfied are you with your living experience at this property?
- What's one thing we could do to improve your experience as a tenant?

This type of listening is about a key part of our core value of Customer First. The goal is that the team is openly talking with the tenants so frequently that there is a strong rapport with the property manager. Thus, when it comes to listening, we try to approach it from as many angles as possible.

One of the most important ways we listen, though, is to our properties themselves through regular inspections. At Coastline Equity, we are a bit different from the rest of our industry—which generally does inspections when the clients ask or charge a fee for inspections. We inspect our properties consistently, usually bimonthly, much more frequently than other companies, so we can "listen" when that building is telling us something.

# PROPERTY MANAGEMENT EXCELLENCE

*Listen to your properties*

For example, a property came into our management. Like many real estate portfolios in California, it was inherited by the next generation of a family, and we had been working with this client for a couple of years leading up to our taking over its management. The property was stuck in probate court for quite some time—and we started visiting the property before we were in the position to take over in preparation for the changeover. Because of this, we quickly discovered that what the current management company and the current engineer were telling the owners and us did not match what we were seeing with our own eyes and expertise. You always need to listen to what a property itself is telling you—not just a written report.

This particular property was built into the Palos Verdes Peninsula hills. What is important to know is the Palos Verdes Peninsula has a unique soil content that is constantly expanding and contracting. In fact, there is a road in Palos Verdes called Portuguese Bend that has huge drops because the area is geologically unstable and the road shifts so much. Landslides move the land by several feet every month.[2]

This complex we were to begin managing was built on that same soil content. There were levels of garages built into the hill, with multiple floors of the buildings sitting on top of those garages. One of the first times we walked the property, we entered into a garage and could immediately see cracked concrete that showed exposed rebar. The existing engineer tried to reassure us: "Don't worry. It's all cosmetic."

I looked at my own team, exchanging knowing glances. We all knew something was wrong—and that this was more than a cosmetic issue. After we obtained a second opinion (they concurred; yes, it was definitely more than cosmetic), we looked more carefully at the property and found another "surprise." The community pool was also above the garages—and it was leaking. In fact, it had probably been leaking, as close as we could figure it, for about fifteen years.

---

2   Emma Tucker, "'Hell No, We're Not Leaving': A California Community Defies Evacuation Warning as Ancient Landslide Rips Their Homes Apart," CNN, September 9, 2024, https://www.cnn.com/2024/09/09/us/rancho-palos-verdes-california-landslide/index.html.

## PROPERTY MANAGEMENT EXCELLENCE

*Removing the failed garage*

## CHAPTER 4

Once we started addressing the pool and involving soil engineers, we discovered more surprises. Water was leaking—from pretty much everywhere. The property was like a sieve. The hillside behind the property was allowing water into the building's structure, plumbing lines had cracked, plus there was the pool issue.

However, the problems at the property were not only soil issues. At the heart of the problem were decades of existing ownership hiring property management firms without a commitment to the principles we discuss in this book. The property was *neglected*. No one was listening when the property was trying to tell them it had issues. Cracked walls and exposed rebar were ignored. Leaking water was ignored—until it became a problem of much bigger proportions.

The management, by not visiting the site, not inspecting, not looking at the problems, not listening, was as responsible—or more responsible—for the problems than the unusual soil.

Since Coastline Equity has taken the helm, not only were the problems fixed, but we also have regular on-site inspections with photos—with time stamps. We do this for all our properties. It was this proactive approach that meant I noticed new ground movement after we had done those repairs on this property, in fact. This was spotted before it could become a disaster. There was about three inches of movement that happened over the course of six months, which shouldn't occur.

We brought the engineers back out, and we found an area of the building that wasn't even on our radar, where water had washed out the soil underneath the garage. We had to rip out that garage and replace it, which was costly; however, if we hadn't caught that, a catastrophe could have occurred. After many millions in repairs and rebuilds later, the property has become a beautiful one, worth the investment several times over.

Another example of our listening and communication commitment occurred when we acquired another property management company that was a slow adopter of proptech. The owners of this company were lovely people—but were antiquated with their systems. Whereas I am committed to efficiencies that technology and documented processes can create, they still had paper and inconsistent processes that needed to be brought into this new era of property tech.

Meanwhile, they had a "No news is good news" approach to inspections. Once a tenant moved in, they never checked on that tenant as long as rent was being paid. They never went inside. When we took over, we reached out to the tenants in our normal proactive approach. We sent notices reminding them how to send in work orders. We received about seven hundred (!) work orders in the first month. Basically, these were all the existing issues that had never been resolved.

Since this portfolio had not been inspected or cared for, as we went through the volumes of work orders, we found mold, water leaks, and failed balconies, among countless other repairs, big and small. There was a unit in one property where, every single rainy season, the water flowed into her and her neighbor's apartments from their balconies. And every year the previous management just cleaned up the water and called it a day. They never addressed the fact that water was flowing into their apartment every year.

But I actually enjoy problem-solving. I always have. Just like I used to pride myself on working with the most difficult kids at the Boys & Girls Club, I like dealing with the most difficult property management cases. Clients who are struggling, clients who come to us with financial issues or structural issues, are the ones from whom I get the most satisfaction helping. When we can take that property from having major cash flow or structural issues into a class-A asset, it is so rewarding. It is gratifying for people who inherit problematic properties to know their future is now secure. I feel like I am making a difference.

Recently, we took on an apartment building where the patriarch passed away, and the matriarch was ill. The property was no longer looked after when she went into the care facility. It was neglected and in disrepair. In fact, it got so bad that the City of Los Angeles stepped in. Like many cities, Los Angeles has a program to protect renters—in this case, it is called the Rent Escrow Account Program (REAP). Tenants no longer paid the landlord—they paid the city until the building's issues were resolved.

The family called us in. We have addressed the issues, are bringing it back to full occupancy, and got it out of the REAP, and now it is back to being a performing asset. It's a win for the tenants. It's a win for the family. It's a win for the community (which is another part of the equation).

As we like to emphasize, if dealing with other people's problems, issues, and stress is not something you get energized about, this isn't the right career for you. But if you like every day being different, putting out fires, and problem-solving, you just might love it.

We will discuss this a little more in chapter 7 on "Quality of Life," but the things that property managers thrive on—that managing of problems I am describing—is the very thing that can cause our managers and people stress. They have to "listen" to complaints and concerns.

You may have heard the analogy of the bucket of rocks. You put the big rocks in first—because those are the most important items (in our business, those are the big projects that are moving your portfolio forward). Then you can fill in your bucket with pebbles—and finally the really small stuff that drives us all crazy: the sand.

We are trying to help our team prioritize, so they can listen to our properties, tenants, and clients (see Figure 4.1).

# PROPERTY MANAGEMENT EXCELLENCE

# TO-DO LIST

**DATE**

**TOP 3 PRIORITIES**
- [ ] ..........................
- [ ] ..........................
- [ ] ..........................

**NOTES**

**TO-DO**
- [ ] ..........................
- [ ] ..........................
- [ ] ..........................
- [ ] ..........................
- [ ] ..........................
- [ ] ..........................
- [ ] ..........................
- [ ] ..........................
- [ ] ..........................
- [ ] ..........................
- [ ] ..........................
- [ ] ..........................
- [ ] ..........................
- [ ] ..........................
- [ ] ..........................
- [ ] ..........................
- [ ] ..........................
- [ ] ..........................

**DAILY ACTIVITIES LIST**
1. Emergencies
2. AppFolio Dashboard
   A. Work orders
   B. Delinquencies
   C. Overdue activities
   D. Move ins and Move out
3. Voicemails
4. E-Mails
5. Work Orders
6. Bills
7. Credit Card Receipts
8. Work Order Labor Summary
9. To-Do List
10. Calendar
11. Inspections

Before the end of your day, it's key that you respond to all phone calls, text messages, and emails that came in during today's business hours.

*Figure 4.1. Prioritizing in Property Management Excellence*

CHAPTER 4

# Communicating in Leadership

I had to learn some leadership lessons the hard way. And I don't mean my story or my difficult upbringing. (Though those taught me leadership skills as well.) I started out, in my early years as CEO, wanting to be accessible to everyone all the time. The last I checked, we cannot yet clone ourselves, and I spread myself much too thin.

Basically, my corporate model was me at the top—and a horizontal line with nearly every employee below me. There was no hierarchy, and though there is something very important about having an open-door policy and being available to your team, the way I was leading was a recipe for burnout.

However, I also was not willing to be in some corner office, out of touch with the people who are so much a part of our success. In the end, tech was, once again, something essential to solving the problem. I now create videos keeping the team informed. I feel quite comfortable on camera, and they are hearing important information and hopefully some inspiration directly from me. They can watch at their own convenience, and it keeps everyone in the loop.

We also shifted to a "pod" style of property management, which required restructuring and altering our approach to teams. The pod model has small, autonomous teams, formed to work on specific portions of our property management portfolio. Each pod operates like a miniteam or minicompany within our larger company. This gives them autonomy—but also accountability.

Pods usually consist of members with diverse skills, enabling them to handle various aspects of the portfolio without relying heavily on external resources (see Figure 4.2). Instead of a traditional hierarchical structure (which I do not embrace, as it is an older style of leadership with a single person at the top), leadership is distributed within the pods. Pods increased our agility. It was tough to look at the bottlenecks at Coastline Equity and realize the bottlenecks were *me*.

## POD SYSTEM PROPERTY MANAGEMENT

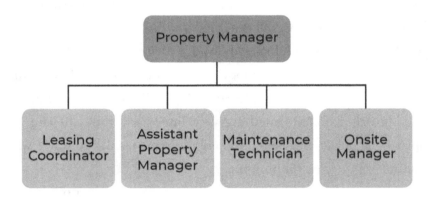

*Figure 4.2. Pod-style leadership*

Now our team can quickly adapt to changes and pivot as needed, making this model well suited for the fast-paced world of property management. Each property manager has a team that supports their pod's goals. Pods encourage communication between each other as well as collaboration. Every week, we have a team meeting with every single person in our company—from porters to leadership. I also have leadership meetings where I can let that team know what's going on in the sales pipeline, which is important so that the human resources team can get ready. We, like many companies, had hiring issues during the pandemic, and postpandemic, we have tried to keep ourselves at peak staffing levels. However, that comes with its own risks.

I also work to stay vigilant about making sure that my team isn't burning out. The industry has a high turnover and burnout rate. Unless you're on vacation, if you are a property manager, you are "on" twenty-four seven, dealing with, as I said, other people's problems. We are hired to deal with tenants' complaints, tenants' issues, tenants' frustrations, and property emergencies, and we do our best work in high-pressure situations. When a main line blows, electricity goes out, or a roof has a massive leak, we thrive on handling it the way we do best.

I remember one time when Lauren and I were new in the industry; we had Disneyland passes. In Southern California, it does not rain very often, and we were in the park when the first big rain of the year came in a deluge. It was the "movie rain," in sheets. I immediately looked at Lauren and said, "We have to go back home."

She looked at me, puzzled. "Why? Nobody's called us yet."

But I knew it was coming. Sure enough, as we started walking back to the parking structure, the calls started.

I looked at Lauren, and we both started laughing (classic knowing your portfolio). Welcome to the world of property management!

## Listening to Your Tenants

It's not uncommon for the relationship between management companies and tenants to become adversarial. As managers, we have a fiduciary responsibility to property owners, but that doesn't mean we're in opposition to tenants. In fact, striking a balance between both parties is key for long-term success.

At Coastline Equity, we don't view tenant relations as a "landlord versus tenant" situation. Instead, we approach it as an opportunity to create value for everyone involved. We train our property managers to understand one key practice that George taught me: be in the middle of challenges and look for solutions that benefit both the owner and the tenant.

## PROPERTY MANAGEMENT EXCELLENCE

In commercial property management, much of the lease is negotiable. For example, a common issue we see is HVAC repair. The lease might stipulate that if the HVAC system breaks down and the repair costs more than 50 percent of a replacement, the landlord has the right to bill the tenant, even though the unit may be decades old. Legally, the landlord might be in the right, but is it fair to make a new tenant, who has been there for less than a year, pay for an outdated system?

A good tenant is an investment in itself, and keeping them satisfied can lead to long-term returns. During the COVID-19 pandemic, we saw how important it was to maintain flexibility in these types of arrangements, especially when both landlords and tenants were facing unprecedented financial stress.

I will discuss it in more detail in the "Ethics and Integrity" chapter, but we have a Renter's Bill of Rights that goes beyond what residential housing requires and goes beyond normal commercial practices. This is good business because we know people see the difference. We have very loyal clients, and we keep growing.

Part of it, though, is listening. We try to be as empathetic as we can and demonstrate to our tenants that we care. We often meet tenants who have had very negative experiences with other management companies. We lead with transparency and tell them how we approach things the Coastline Equity way. When we present tenants with this Renter's Bill of Rights, we inform them that they can expect these things from us. And if they don't receive those rights, we want them to tell us. We want them to raise the alarm, and we will immediately address it.

In addition, as our next section demonstrates, listening does not mean avoiding the difficult conversations. I will share how we make communications, even over conflicts, productive.

CHAPTER 4

# Listening and Transforming Conflict: The Equity Approach in Action

I believe property management excellence means building thriving communities where everyone feels heard, respected, and empowered. This includes navigating the inevitable challenges of tenant conflict with empathy and a commitment to win-win solutions.

As I have said, property management is about dealing with other people's problems and stresses. Conflict is unavoidable—and the property managers are in the middle. We must have an owner mindset because of our fiduciary and ethical obligations, but the tenants have rights as well.

For us, it's not about avoiding tough conversations; it's about transforming them into opportunities for positive change. Remember the owners and property managers I mentioned who had a "No news is good news" approach to inspections? If you are managing properties as an owner, or you have property managers, avoiding inspections means you are merely putting off the difficult conversations—and expenses—down the road when a small problem may very well have grown. We want to know the problems early on—before they snowball into big ones.

The Coastline Equity Approach we developed is a framework for fostering positive relationships and achieving mutually beneficial outcomes, even in challenging situations.

# The Problem with the "Red Zone"

I tell our team, as I have said, that our job is to deal with other people's property problems. And problems don't make anyone happy. But it is also important to remember that for tenants, it's *personal*. It is where they live or work—or with today's hybrid and work-from-home situations, it's both! When a tenant is angry, our initial reaction can often escalate the situation. We enter the "Red Zone," a reactive mindset that hinders resolution.

> **RED ZONE WARNING SIGNS**
>
> - **Adversarial dynamics:** We view the tenant as an opponent instead of a valued customer or community member, creating an "us versus them" mentality. This is why we like finding people enthusiastic about property management, even if they are newer to the business. We want the problem solvers, those with compassion along with a sense of responsibility to the owners; we want team players and collaborators.
> - **Blame and justification:** In the Red Zone, conversations become defensive, focusing on proving our point rather than understanding their perspective. This is never helpful and mires the conversation further. It means we don't listen and instead just react.
> - **Quick fixes, deeper issues:** In the Red Zone, we rush to find a Band-Aid solution, neglecting the underlying causes and creating potential for future conflict. In terms of quick fixes, think of the example of the flooding apartments where the real problem was never addressed.

Our method of communication avoids the Red Zone and deescalates the situation.

> **Property Management Excellence Tip:**
>
> Band-Aids only lead to problems down the road. Find the root cause; find the source of the problem.

# The Equity Approach: Building Bridges, Not Walls

The Equity Approach framework (see Figure 4.3) shifts the paradigm from confrontation to collaboration, emphasizing empathy, respect, and a genuine desire for mutually beneficial outcomes. The relationship between the tenant, property manager, and property owner never has to be adversarial. I saw, in my own childhood, how property managers would especially avoid dealing with the concerns of the poor. No matter who the tenant is or what kind of property it is, everyone should be accorded respect.

We teach our teams to:

1. **Recognize the individual:** Before entering the conversation, remind yourself that you are interacting with a person with their own unique story, challenges, and aspirations. Separate the individual from the issue at hand.

2. **Practice active listening:** Go beyond simply hearing their words; listen for the emotions and unmet needs driving their concerns. Ask clarifying questions to demonstrate genuine interest and ensure understanding.

3. **Empower through collaboration:** Instead of dictating solutions, invite their input and cocreate a resolution. Ask, "What are your thoughts on how we might address this?" or "What would a positive outcome look like for you?" Ultimately, there are lease agreements that need to be honored and enforced, but many times there is room for collaboration and a mutually beneficial resolution.

4. **Value their perspective:** Even when opinions differ or their request cannot be met, recognize the value in their unique viewpoint. Thank them for sharing their thoughts and acknowledge how their perspective contributes to finding a resolution.

5. **Realize that respect is paramount:** Treat every individual with dignity and respect, regardless of their emotional state or the nature of the conflict. Maintain a calm and professional demeanor throughout the interaction, using respectful language and a solution-oriented tone.

# CHAPTER 4

# THE EQUITY APPROACH

**The Equity Approach** is a unique property management approach developed by Coastline Equity. It focuses on **building strong, collaborative relationships** between landlords and tenants, optimizing financial performance, and satisfying stakeholders.

Coastline Equity's Equity Approach is based on the following **key steps:**

1. Recognize the individual
2. Practice active listening
3. Empower through collaboration
4. Value other perspectives
5. Respect is non-negotiable

*Figure 4.3. The Equity Approach framework*

Handled this way, with real listening, which is part of our DNA, the conflict can be deescalated. If someone feels as if their complaints and concerns are being *heard,* that alone can often lessen tension. This allows the two parties to find common ground—to find the win-win. This also strengthens trust in the communities we serve.

This is how we redefine excellence in property management—one interaction at a time. These principles can be used right now in your own property management approach.

> **Property Management Excellence Tip:**
>
> **Do not wait to have difficult conversations. Keep communications open all the time—and look for additional channels and methods, including the latest in tech, to ensure they feel heard.**

# Listening to the Community and the World

Like every leader, I have a COVID-19 story on how we adapted and how we got through. Here again, communication and listening were at its heart.

For property managers, it pays to plan for the worst, hope for the best—but always have a plan. Fortunately, I have always had that trait. I was working with a potential client, a Singapore-based developer. In early 2020, we were having many late-night calls because of the time difference. China started having the murmurs of this virus in January or February, and Singapore wasn't far behind China. I remember being on a call with this developer and asking him, "What are you hearing over there?"

He responded, "It's getting bad. Get ready."

When I asked him what he meant, he mentioned that they could no longer find masks—in many Asian cultures, people who are sick have been masking for years. I asked him if it was spreading. He said, "It's everywhere," but at the time, his government was not talking about it publicly yet.

As someone who plans for the worst, I told my leadership team at the next meeting that we needed a plan—but I don't think any of us could have known what we would soon be up against. However, I remember telling my assistant at the time, who was great with technology and really helped me with all our technology implementation, that we needed to develop our game plan for this potential pandemic. We already had a voice-over IP system. We already had digital phones, but we didn't have equipment at people's homes. Most of our staff didn't have laptops. So we examined our tech and determined how we would operate from home.

When COVID-19 finally reached our shores and the lockdowns began, everyone on our team was pretty worried about how we would operate the company. But my assistant and I assured them all that we had already figured it all out. We distributed the plan to everyone. When everyone went home the night before the lockdown in LA, which was probably the strictest one in the country at the time, we just followed our process. It was like turning on a switch—we were good to go.

Soon our phones were ringing like crazy from tenants concerned about not being able to pay rent. For many commercial tenants, their businesses essentially disappeared overnight and with little warning. George and I took the list of all of our commercial tenants, and we broke up the list. He and I, between us, in the first couple of days of COVID-19, called every single commercial tenant and reassured them that we knew what their businesses were going through. There was a whole mantra of "We're in this together"—and we meant it.

Our commitment to doing what was right guided us. As third-party property managers, we had to get client agreement and buy-in first, and that is what we did. Then we set about making plans and lease amendments. We assured tenants that if they could not pay rent, to pay their staff. (Obviously, if they could pay their rent, we wanted them to.) In the early days, we offered payment plans to tenants so they would not accrue late fees. We even helped tenants in more practical ways. For example, if any restaurants were not on Uber Eats or Grubhub, we gave them advice for how to get set up and use it as a new, temporary business model.

On the other side, with the clients, we explained that it would be favorable to try to work this out with their tenants. We encouraged them to renegotiate lease terms or provide abatements or rent relief if it was even possible.

Then the government offered the Paycheck Protection Program (PPP) through the Coronavirus Aid, Relief, and Economic Security (CARES) Act, designed to help small businesses by providing eight weeks of payroll, including benefits costs. When these loans started, we went back to the tenants and reminded them of their delayed rent or abatement and worked with them to ensure the owners and clients also were treated fairly during those unprecedented times.

We were proactive with both sides of the property management equation, which starts with listening.

Listening is also about looking around your community and seeing the positive changes you can make. We maintain our commercial properties in such a way that tenants are safe and happy and feel good about where they work—which means the clients have a more profitable, valuable asset.

# CHAPTER 4

> **Property Management Excellence Tip:**
>
> When property managers invest their time, money, talents, and interest in a community, the rewards are beyond just dollars. It creates communities we all want to live and work in.

# Pay It Forward

I always admired George's commitment to give 2 percent of his top-line revenue to causes he believed in. In our area, he is a legendary philanthropist. When Lauren and I took over Coastline Equity in 2022, we announced to the team that George was retiring at the holiday party that year. After he gave a very moving speech and symbolically passed the baton, Lauren and I shared what was next for the business.

I announced to George and to the team that Lauren and I had agreed that we were going to donate 50 percent of net profits every year to nonprofits that not only Lauren and I feel strongly about and that fit our core values, but also that the staff feels strongly about, and that we would match any of their donations.

George and I had always swapped speeches before any speaking event, so we could each give the other edits or comments. This time when we had swapped speeches, I gave him a hard time and said, "I'm going to cry when you give this speech, and you're going to cry."

> **Property Management Excellence Tip:**
>
> Not every gift has to be monetary. You can give of your time, talent, and treasure. What's important is impacting your team, business, and community in a positive way.

As he read through mine, he said, "Wait, is this a typo? You're going to give 50 percent of your profits to charity?"

I know it sounds outside the box and ambitious—but I have never backed away from challenges. When you embrace a tenet of listening, then you also embrace this idea of contributing to the greater good. Lauren and I have always had this mindset, even before we were married or owned a business together. When we were still colleagues working in the nonprofit space, we started to realize there were people around us really making a difference through philanthropy.

We met another entrepreneurial couple at an event one evening, and I think they were the ones who planted the seed of aiming for big giving. They talked about the work that they were doing, a sports organization; they were very passionate about building sustainable sports courts and tennis courts, soccer pitches, and baseball fields and doing it in a way that teaches the community how to maintain it and turn that into a business of their own. Lauren and I really liked their ambition about charity. She and I both have different passions when it comes to nonprofits, but we looked at the things that we could be passionate about together.

For us, those passions are youth development, equity and tolerance, access to housing, access to economic development, and the arts. I think both because of my background and upbringing and my experience with mentors and the Boys & Girls Club, and with Lauren being a social worker, again, we've always felt drawn to those issues. We do the work we do in real estate and in investment management because we love it, but also because of the freedom it gives us to support the organizations that we care about. We can sit on nonprofit boards and work on local committees and can still be very involved in the work that means the most to us.

## Ways for You to Engage with Your Community

If you have also given thought on how you can give back in your own community but wonder where to start, here are some suggestions:

- **Fund local educational programs:** Support local schools, provide scholarships, or sponsor after-school programs to improve educational access and opportunities.

- **Invest in affordable housing:** Contribute to or start initiatives that create affordable housing, reducing homelessness and housing insecurity in the community. (We will discuss this later in the book.)

- **Support local health services:** Donate to community hospitals, clinics, or mental health services, improving access to quality healthcare for all residents.

- **Sponsor small business development:** Provide grants or low-interest loans to local entrepreneurs, helping them start or grow businesses that contribute to the local economy. Mentor people looking to start their first businesses.

- **Fund community arts and culture:** Support local artists, theaters, and cultural institutions, ensuring the arts thrive and are accessible to everyone.

- **Create or support food security programs:** Donate to food banks, or fund community gardens and initiatives aimed at reducing hunger.

- **Support environmental sustainability projects:** Fund local projects focused on green spaces, clean energy, recycling programs, beach or park cleanups, or conservation efforts.

- **Mentorship and workforce development:** Provide mentorship programs or fund training initiatives that prepare local residents for high-demand jobs and better career opportunities.

- **Sponsor youth and recreational programs:** This one is close to my own heart. Invest in community centers, sports programs, and other recreational activities that engage youth and provide safe, positive environments.

- **Fund social justice and equality initiatives:** Support non-profits and initiatives working to reduce inequality, promote diversity, and address systemic issues in the community.

These actions can drive long-term positive change, improving the overall quality of life in their communities.

All of this is possible through a commitment to listening. Now our next essential tenet is *Ethics and Integrity in All We Do.*

# CHAPTER 5

## Ethics and Integrity in All We Do

---

*Integrity is doing the right thing, even when no one is watching.*
—C. S. LEWIS

---

The mentors I met at the Boys & Girls Club shaped my understanding of what it means to live with purpose and integrity. They gave their time and energy to improve the lives of kids who needed someone to believe in them. Their example stayed with me as I grew older and encountered people on very different paths. People like George, who embodied integrity and worked to make a difference, reinforced the belief that living with principles mattered.

Before we move into our chapter on ethics and integrity, let's define both. Ethics is a set of principles or rules that govern behavior based on what is considered right or wrong by society, an organization, or a profession. It involves guidelines that help people determine how they should act in various situations (which you will see an example of in our next section on the Renter's Bill of Rights).

Ethical standards can vary depending on the context, such as professional ethics (e.g., medical ethics, legal ethics, and in this chapter, ethics in property management) versus personal ethics. What is considered ethical in one culture or profession may not be viewed the same way in another.

Integrity, on the other hand, refers to the quality of being honest, consistent, and trustworthy, adhering to moral and ethical principles in one's actions and decisions. It is about maintaining consistency among your beliefs, values, and behavior.

Ethics tends to focus only on behavior. So if someone works for a company and operates with a set of professional ethics within that corporation and profession, that guides their behavior. But *inside*, or away from their job, that person might cheat on their spouse, or be deeply unkind. However, their professional ethics may be impeccable.

Integrity *is* the inside. It focuses on character—the kind of person someone is and whether they consistently act according to their values. Not only that—and this is hugely important—but integrity is also what you do and who you are when no one else is watching.

We expect ethics and integrity in medicine—after all, we are entrusting our doctors with our lives and our private health histories. We are entrusting them with our families and loved ones. We expect ethics and integrity in many professions, like teaching and the law. For us at Coastline Equity, it is a cornerstone of how we deal with everyone from tenants to investors, from our team to tradespeople and others who work on our properties—in everything we do. After all, we are dealing with people's assets—and with tenants' lives and workplaces.

CHAPTER 5

# The Renter's Bill of Rights

As I mentioned in the previous chapter, we have a Renter's Bill of Rights (see Figure 5.1), which is given to every renter we have, spelling out our commitments to them. What Lauren and I found as we took leadership of Coastline is that we initially had property managers who weren't treating residents like residents. They weren't unethical people. However, their background and experience were more in the commercial sector of the industry—and while we lean heavily commercial as well, we also have multifamily residential properties. For those people, issues pertaining to their residence, as I said in the section on the Red Zone in the previous chapter, it is personal. This is their home. But some property managers were treating it more like their business office.

Meanwhile, just before and then during the COVID-19 pandemic, there was a flurry of news articles in the media about unscrupulous property managers. For example, an elderly woman had died in her apartment during a heat wave because the property manager had ignored the broken HVAC. After seeing this—and feeling disheartened by my own industry—I published an article[3] that was meant to be a call to action for the property management industry as a whole. We needed, as a group, to weed out our own bad apples and start setting a standard for ourselves as an industry before the government and other entities passed more regulations that would not take us in the direction we needed to go—and probably would not solve the problems.

What we needed was a Renter's Bill of Rights.

---

3   Anthony A. Luna, "The Need for a Renter's Bill of Rights," *Forbes,* January 26, 2023, https://www.forbes.com/councils/forbesbusinesscouncil/2023/01/26/the-need-for-a-renters-bill-of-rights/#:~:text=A%20renter's%20bill%20of%20rights%20should.

After all, it is the people in an industry who know the problems best. We know the pitfalls, the unexpected crises that could arise, as well as all the moving parts and stakeholders.

At the time, I was dealing with the perception of the industry—and it was not a positive one. It was also at a time where across the country we were experiencing the "Great Resignation." People, with the stresses of COVID-19, began questioning their jobs and their lives—confronted with death tolls and the immense difficulties of the pandemic, many decided to change course. Some turned their side hustles into businesses; others just decided they wanted to simplify their lives. In a climate where people were being very choosy about accepting jobs, I wanted our industry to attract the best people—and we could never do that with a reputation that was faltering.

I spent some time thinking of the issues at hand, and I created our Renter's Bill of Rights. I rolled it out first to my leadership team, asking them what we needed to add or change. Next we took it to the whole company. Since at the time we were remote, we did our all-hands meeting on Zoom—and then we did breakout sessions to fine-tune the document. I wanted to be sure everything we stood for was there, that no parts were impractical or would lead to miscommunications with the tenants. In the end, we had a document we believed in and were proud of—one unique in our industry.

While details may change as our industry advances, the general elements of a Renter's Bill of Rights include those shown in the illustration.

CHAPTER 5

# COASTLINE EQUITY RENTER'S BILL OF RIGHTS

**Tenants' issues** → **Actions to be taken** → **Tenants' rights**

Tenants encounter issues like unfair evictions, unsafe living conditions, or unregulated rent increases.

The landlord can establish clear policies, conduct inspections, provide fair leases, and comply with local housing regulations.

Rights such as rent control, the right to reparations, or laws protecting against evictions without just cause are created.

- **Right to an Equal Opportunity to Apply**
    - Efficient Application Timeline
    - Efficient Move-In Timeline
    - Clear Application Criteria
    - Response Regarding Approval, Denial, or Cancellation
- **Right to Effective Shelter/Business Operations**
    - Habitability or Effective Business Location
    - Repairs Resolved Within 48 Hours
    - Temperature Control (Geographically Based on Air Conditioning)
    - Quiet Enjoyment
- **Right to Respectful Communication**
    - Listen to Our Tenants' Concerns
    - Response Within the Same Business Day to All Forms of Communication
    - Empathy for Our Tenants' Views
- **Right to Positive Credit Reporting**
    - Reporting Positive Reporting to the Credit Bureaus
    - Access to Credit Reporting
- **Right to Clear Move-Out Requirements**
    - Move Out Requirements Prepared and Delivered at Lease Signing
    - Disposition Within 21 Days
    - Clear Dispute Process for Disposition Letter

*Figure 5.1. The Coastline Equity Renter's Bill of Rights*

These are basic rights that we should all expect of a place we choose to live or work. Our own Renter's Bill of Rights goes *beyond* the regulations and laws governing us in California. As I said early in the book, I *lived* in Section 8 housing throughout San Pedro, and now I have also worked in the property management world for years and run my own company—I've seen the good and the bad. But my personal ethics and integrity—and those of my team—dictate that we do more because it is the right thing to do.

In fact, this QR code will take you to our most current Bill of Rights for our renters—for other property managers, consider something similar!

## Same-Day Response

Same-day response is something very important to our company as well. To me, it demonstrates a commitment to the tenant—that we care. And we do!

To be clear, a same-day response may not mean a tenant's non-emergency repair is fixed instantly (I wish it were that easy). But a same-day response does mean they will hear back from us indicating their issue has been noted, and they will learn what we will be doing to resolve it. Once again, technology helps us with that and will only improve as advancements in artificial intelligence and smart systems develop more efficiencies.

A same-day response from a landlord or their property manager is important for several reasons:

- **Urgency of repairs:** Some issues, such as plumbing leaks, electrical problems, or heating failures, require immediate attention to prevent further damage or health hazards. Every year, there are tragic stories of the elderly or vulnerable people passing in too-hot or too-cold apartments, and weather extremes are increasing. Not only is handling urgent repairs essential for the tenant, but it is also important to prevent any structural or cosmetic damages to the property. (We will talk in the next chapter about the "owner mindset" and our responsibilities to our investors and property owners.)

- **Safety concerns:** Tenants may face safety issues, such as broken locks or windows, which need prompt resolution to ensure their security. Prompt attention to safety is especially important in common areas as well, such as stairwells or parking lots. Slip-and-fall accidents and other safety-related lawsuits can arise when issues are neglected.

- **Tenant satisfaction:** Quick responses show that the landlord values the tenant's comfort and concerns, fostering a positive landlord-tenant relationship. You may recall in the previous chapter in the section on "Listening to Our Properties" that tenants will let you know what they like about a property—and when they leave, they will often tell you why. Same-day response is something all tenants can appreciate. For landlords, addressing issues quickly can prevent loss of rental income due to uninhabitable conditions or tenant dissatisfaction, leading to vacancies.

- **Prevention of escalation:** Addressing problems promptly can prevent minor issues from escalating into major, more costly repairs. We do our biweekly/frequent inspections precisely to avoid this. We want to know when problems are manageable—not at crisis levels.

For Coastline Equity, same-day response is just part of our proactive approach. With our nonadversarial approach to our tenants and our commitment to our owners and investors, this policy is a win-win for all.

# Repairs and Maintenance Done Right

The world was shocked by the 2021 Surfside condominium collapse. There was and is plenty of blame to go around for the disaster.[4] It caused the death of nearly a hundred people, and the repercussions are still being felt as older buildings are being inspected for the same sorts of issues.

Property management excellence means repairs should be done correctly. Shortcuts may seem like they are saving time and money in the short run, but for the long term, property investment is an asset that is often generational, and doing it right means protecting that investment for years and decades to come.

Unethical property managers may try to take shortcuts when it comes to building repairs, often prioritizing cost savings or convenience over the well-being and satisfaction of tenants.

Some of these shortcuts include:

---

4   Patricia Mazzei et al., "Search for Clues in Miami Collapse Focuses on a Key Element: The Building's Foundation," *New York Times*, June 27, 2021, https://www.nytimes.com/2021/06/27/us/miami-building-investigation-clues.html.

- **Using unlicensed or inexperienced contractors:** Hiring unlicensed or underqualified contractors to perform repairs can be cheaper, but it often results in poor-quality work that may not meet safety or cosmetic standards. Believe me, if you have ever seen Sheetrock hung wrong, you would know what I mean. We want our repairs done right the first time—and we give our people the support, tools, and training to ensure that happens.

- **Band-Aid solutions:** Instead of addressing the root cause of a problem, unethical property managers might apply temporary fixes that only mask the issue temporarily, such as patching over leaks without fixing the underlying plumbing problem. I've seen properties where mold was just painted over. There's a reason why often, on those home makeover shows, when the contractors tear down a wall, they find lots of "surprises" like shoddy wiring, mold, plumbing leaks, and the like. Like the apartment building that simply cleaned up the water that leaked in each rainy season, this is a shortsighted "solution."

- **Low-quality materials or substandard parts:** Unethical managers might use the cheapest available materials for repairs. For critical systems like plumbing or electrical work, using substandard parts can cause more significant issues down the line.

- **Prioritizing costs over comfort:** Poorly run property management companies might delay repairs that aren't immediately life-threatening, such as fixing leaks or broken appliances, to save money. Again, for tenants, this is personal. If one toilet in a two-bedroom, two-bath apartment isn't working, that creates a real issue for the people living there, as does having to stick a pot under a leaky ceiling every time it rains.

Are these things crises? No, but they are not comfortable, and they impact how a tenant feels about their home. For commercial clients, it's personal too. We all can think of a time where we walked out of a restaurant or store because the temperature was uncomfortably hot, or pulled away from a shopping center because the parking lot was poorly maintained and rutted and weedy.

- **No quality control:** As I have written elsewhere, Coastline Equity does consistent inspections with time-stamped photos. This not only lets us see problems before they become *huge* problems, but after a repair is completed, it is important to have follow-up inspections to ensure the work was done correctly. This is often overlooked by property managers looking to cut corners and leaves tenants to deal with any ongoing issues.

> **Property Management Excellence Tip:**
>
> Doing repairs right means taking the time and the care, with the right materials, to do it perfectly the first time. In the end, that is more cost-effective (measure seven times, cut once, as the adage goes) and makes for happier tenants and a better-cared-for property.

# Kickbacks and Gifts

In our next chapter, we will talk about needing an "owner mindset" when you are a property manager. We must put our fiduciary responsibility to the client first. Our client's financials are most important. But a common problem in the industry is property management companies creating a situation where it is actually more advantageous for them to find the most expensive bid because either they're going to get a kickback or they're going to get a portion of the maintenance cost.

Some (in fact, most) property management companies charge a percentage on every maintenance service. So if the property management company must send a plumber, they will charge a 5 percent fee to manage that plumber. In my opinion, the property manager's and the client's interests are no longer aligned. The property manager is disincentivized to find the cheapest bid.

Unless the property manager is getting a direct kickback, where it is a quid-pro-quo situation, that scenario is completely legal. However, there are still people who do a form of the quid pro quo and pick a vendor because they are going to get a kickback that's not documented.

To try to avoid such conflicts of interest, consider, as we do, always getting a minimum of three bids for any jobs over a set amount. In addition, we have a strict policy on accepting gifts from tenants or vendors. Consider a commercial tenant who might give one of our employees expensive tickets to a Lakers game, for example. When that tenant calls for an urgent repair, will our employee prioritize the Lakers-gift-giver over someone else? Everyone must be treated equally.

## The Care and Feeding of Our Properties

We have these core principles of how we treat our tenants and how we treat our properties, but it all works together. All the stories I share fundamentally come down to how we care for our properties. I would not ask someone to invest with me if I am not going to take care of them and their real estate portfolio or their investment with us.

## PROPERTY MANAGEMENT EXCELLENCE

My team is going to baby this property better than anybody because we have developed these processes—and we have made ethics and integrity in *everything* we do core to who we are.

But a "property" is much more than a building. It is an investment, an asset. And it is a *home* or a place of work for people. And we want to especially care for those people and where they work and play with ethics and integrity as well.

Some examples of ethics and integrity woven through the whole of property management excellence include:

- For us, we help our teams prioritize their daily roles and responsibilities. It is the care of our people that means trying to avoid burnout (we will discuss this more in our "Quality of Life" chapter).

- Clarity about move-in and move-out—clear communication helps ensure integrity.

- Inspecting properties correctly, including watermarks, time, day, and geographical location. That ensures those doing the inspections are held to a high degree of integrity—and that our clients can therefore trust our inspections are completely ethical, with proof.

These are just a few examples—it is never about one piece. It is the holistic approach.

Ethics and integrity should be the bedrocks of property management and investing.

# CHAPTER 6

## Owner Mindset

> *The success of a vision is determined by its ownership by both the leader and the people.*
> —JOHN C. MAXWELL

I've spoken of an owner mindset before, but now we will look at what that means in a little more detail.

For us, we sit down with new clients as we're signing the contract, and we want to understand their mindset. What are their goals? What are their needs for the property? What do they want done with the property? Because our approach to managing it is going to change based on what their goals are. We have to think with their best interests and goals in mind.

One client might need us to be a caretaker of this property because they're going to sell it in twelve months because they need the money to finance the owner's retirement. In that case, we are not going to recommend a major renovation plan or a new roof. We will maintain it properly and in the right way—but the strategy is different.

Our owner mindset is what each individual client needs. If you are in the world of property management, always ask, What are my client's goals with this property? What is the business/management plan?

It will not be (or should not be) a one-size-fits-all approach.

The second component of having an owner mindset is considering growth for yourself and your team. That concern for growth applies not just to growing the company's valuation but also to growing its people and teams, growing its investors and their profits, and growing knowledge each and every day.

Personally, I've always invested in expanding my thinking. Whether through entrepreneurial groups, professional organizations, boards, or councils, I aim to learn not just what others in property management are doing but also how to think outside the box. For instance, how do we future-proof our business to serve the community better or tackle the deepening affordable housing crisis? These are the bigger questions that drive growth—not for growth's sake, but to build something that benefits all stakeholders.

To give an example, regarding the issues of homelessness and affordable housing, the property management industry seems to be running in the opposite direction of the solution, but I see it differently. Just as we created the Renter's Bill of Rights to instill ethics and fairness in tenant treatment, we need to have a seat at the table when it comes to homelessness and affordable housing. Unfortunately, many property managers don't see this as our responsibility, so they avoid the conversation. But I believe this lack of involvement has contributed to a knowledge gap between property managers, government agencies, and nonprofits trying to solve these crises.

At Coastline Equity, we actively participate in LA's homelessness working groups. Right now, we are the only property management company in these discussions. It's a challenge but also a responsibility. Property managers are key to creating viable solutions—whether it's reducing the time for a Section 8 application to be processed, which can take nine months to a year, or improving the actual systems for getting people off the streets and into housing.

We're proud of our role in these efforts. My wife, Lauren, serves on the board of Harbor Connects, an organization that bridges the gap for individuals and families in immediate risk of homelessness. We also participate in the annual nationwide homelessness count because, as property managers, we need to be hands-on in understanding and addressing the challenges in our communities.

These commitments aren't just about the future of Coastline but also the future and growth of the city we call home. As I have written, we all live, work, and play in the same city. It should be a place of opportunity and fairness for all. That's why I encourage other property management companies to get involved in these types of initiatives.

Now we will discuss one of the cornerstones of property management.

## Owner Mindset

As I wrote, our approach is driven by a legal and fiduciary responsibility to treat each property as if it were our own. This "owner mindset" is essential, but it varies depending on each client's goals. Generally, though, this mindset emphasizes long-term value creation, cost-effective management, tenant satisfaction, and preserving or increasing the property's market value. In practical terms, this means:

- **Long-term thinking:** Property management isn't about quick wins or cutting corners—it's about ensuring the long-term health and value of the property. Many of our clients view their portfolios as generational wealth, passing assets from one generation to the next. With this in mind, a property manager with an "owner mindset" prioritizes preventive maintenance and regular inspections to avoid costly repairs down the line. We invest in upkeep, making sure each property stands the test of time, ensuring steady appreciation while minimizing future expenses.

- **Financial prudence:** I am often shocked by how many new clients tell me that their last property manager never showed them the bids for work they had done or statements with charges and costs they had no idea about. Financial prudence and transparency are nonnegotiable. This means cost-effective management, making decisions that balance cost with quality to maximize return on investment (ROI).

- **Maximizing revenue and minimizing vacancies:** An owner mindset means continuously looking for ways to optimize rental income, minimize vacancies, and ensure high occupancy rates. Part of our whole philosophy of caring for our tenants works hand in hand with this because tenants who feel heard and valued tend to stay.

- **Tenant-centric approach:** Our Renter's Bill of Rights demonstrates how we embrace this concept. Understanding that tenant satisfaction directly impacts property performance, an owner mindset means we work to provide excellent customer service, address complaints promptly, and foster a positive living environment. This goes back to listening and communication, to our ethics and integrity, to our belief that we treat everyone with respect.

We prioritize tenant retention through fair lease terms, responsive maintenance, and recognize that long-term tenants are more cost-effective than constantly finding new ones.

- **Asset protection:** For our clients, their real estate portfolio represents one of their most significant assets. As such, those assets must be protected. An owner mindset includes proactive risk management, such as ensuring the property is adequately insured, complies with all regulations, and has up-to-date safety measures. Most importantly, regular inspections and monitoring ensure the property remains in good condition, avoiding neglect that could lead to devaluation. While I included a couple of stories of properties we took over that had not been well cared for, I could have included many more. (And again, those tend to be my pet projects! I love a challenge.)

- **Value-driven decisions:** Property managers must think like owners and make decisions with the property's long-term value in mind, such as choosing quality over the cheapest option and considering how each action impacts the overall property value. When we evaluate renovations, upgrades, or landscaping, we ask ourselves, "How will this improve the property's appeal and market value?" Whether it's high-end apartments or affordable housing, I always ask myself, Would I want to live here? Would I allow my family or friends to live here? If the answer is no, we make it right.

- **Market awareness:** As CEO, it's my job to follow market trends. On my LinkedIn, I often vlog and write about changes in the Southern California markets and trends I see in property values, in areas undergoing revitalization, happenings in waterfront development, etc. An owner-minded property manager must be informed about local real estate market trends, adjusting strategies to ensure the property remains competitive and profitable. Understanding how macroeconomic trends and local development affect our properties helps us protect and enhance their value.

- **Accountability and transparency:** I am often surprised when clients tell me that their previous property managers lacked accountability. Just as an owner would expect transparency, this mindset includes providing clear, detailed reports on property performance, expenses, and any issues.

- **Community and reputation building:** An owner-minded approach often involves building strong relationships with tenants, vendors, and the local community, enhancing the property's reputation and desirability. And then, there is one of my favorite topics, community impact. How does the property fit into and contribute to the local community, understanding that a positive community presence can enhance property value?

- **Efficiency and innovation:** When I initially went to work with George, I was bringing my technological acumen to help get the proptech software working smoothly. Since then, more innovations have come on the scene—and more are coming with the advent of AI and large language models. The owner mindset includes continually seeking ways to improve efficiency in property management operations, whether through technology, better vendor relationships, or improved workflows. Leveraging modern proptech tools for things like maintenance tracking, tenant communication, and energy management is a hallmark of an owner-minded manager, ensuring the property operates at peak efficiency.

Adopting an owner mindset helps property managers make decisions that align with the interests of property owners, leading to better-managed properties, happier tenants, and more successful investment outcomes. For property management excellence, consider how you are ensuring your property owners' goals are being met. How are you tailoring your management objectives for each portfolio?

## Real Estate Investing Growth

The growth mindset I have also extends to my approach to real estate investing, which is a strong direction Coastline Equity is moving toward for the future. I have created investment opportunities for my clients. This is called, in our business, "syndication."

Syndication, the short explanation, is a way for a group of investors to pool their investment money in purchases of commercial real estate. The investors contribute to funding the purchase, whether that is a multifamily property or a large commercial building. The syndicator (or general partner) acquires the asset and manages and runs the properties, as well as oversees renovations or updates to improve the property. The investors are passive partners.

During the COVID-19 era, I was a partner in Coastline Equity with George, and I was doing deals for my clients, but I was not able to invest myself. George and I reinvested every dollar back into the business, which meant I was living on a paycheck and not taking distributions. I could *find* the deals but not be part of them.

Then I came across a property that was an incredible opportunity. I ran the numbers a hundred times—but I knew I could not finance it myself (and I was frustrated by that). I was at one of my entrepreneur groups, at my EO forum, and we were on a break, and I was telling a real estate investor on the passive side about this property. I explained the numbers, what I envisioned for the renovation, and the ROI.

He looked at me and said, "So we're not doing this deal because why?"

I explained I did not have the cash flow to invest at that time. But then he smiled and said that the "we're" meant me and him. He offered to back my deal with the funding; I would handle the heavy lifting, the acquisition, the renovations, and the management of it all, and we would split the profits fifty-fifty.

It didn't feel real, as I explained to Lauren that night. That had not been my intent in discussing the property with him. It felt somewhat like running into George at that dinner and then becoming a partner; it felt like I had to pinch myself. I did trust this investor—and he remains a friend to this day. As I talked it over with Lauren, my brother-in-law happened to be over at the house. He suddenly said he wanted to invest as well. Then Lauren showed me, in our own finances, where we could pull cash from, some savings we had set aside. We *could* invest with partners. I called my friend back and said we would do the deal together.

My ROI projections were spot-on. In fact, it went even better than we could have expected. We had some delays because of COVID-19. Those delays held back our listing date, and the longer that was, the more the market was running hot. In that respect, we were lucky.

Though the pandemic was awful, there were some wild turns in the real estate market.

More importantly, I gained some experience putting my first real syndication together that I was a part of. I ran that deal the way I run Coastline. I try to come from a place with our clients and with my investors, where I am an open book. I essentially say, "Here are all the reports. This is exactly what's happening month to month. Here are the receipts."

I think I also learned that your own money is the way you should be starting to prove your track record when it comes to real estate investment and syndication. I did it for myself, for my family, and my friends first. I did it to grow our financial future—and I took that risk. I think when you're doing passive investing in a syndication, if you ever come across a deal where the operators of that deal, the general partners, don't have their own money in the deal, it's a red flag.

In the business, I see many syndicators with large acquisition fees and no actual dollars on the line. I have also seen people invest in syndication that are located in tertiary markets. For a while, these markets tend to do very well with large returns on investments, but real estate is fickle in tertiary markets, and when it shifts, investors can find themselves upside down.

I have even been to a capital-raising conference where a single syndicator with hundreds of investors lost every single dollar of his investors' money, and all the properties were taken back by the bank. His plan was to move to a new market and start over. He was, sadly, not the only one who "churned and burned" through investors.

I could never do that. Coastline Equity plans to be around for a long, long time. It has been established since 1972. When it comes to investing in commercial real estate, it is good to keep these factors in mind:

- Location, location, location
- Market trends
- Property type
- Tenant quality
- Lease terms
- Financing
- Risk assessment
- Maintenance costs
- Resale value/ROI
- Property management

Being thorough in your due diligence and having a clear understanding of your financial goals and risk tolerance are crucial to success—and trusting your syndicator (and property management company!).

I have a cautionary tale of a client who invested for years in single-tenant commercial buildings. These are usually great investments because the tenant takes care of all the costs of upkeep, taxes, and insurance, and the investor has cash flow. This particular client self-managed his portfolio, but when he invested in a large multitenant park, it was a different story.

His portfolio became too large to manage, so he hired us after one of our real estate contacts referred him to us. At our first meeting, I looked at the numbers and instantly understood that the broker he was buying it from was one who always listed his properties way above market and scrubbed his pro formas. This simply means his deals on paper always look perfect because they are based on a perfect world if everything went right and there were no repairs, no failed HVACs, and no emergency work orders. And when does that ever happen?

Pro formas never consider capital expenses, like renovations, or tenant improvement costs for new tenants. They never envision lease commissions to the brokers who bring those deals. And never ever does a pro forma list property management fees. Thus, your monthly recurring management cost is not included in the pro forma.

I had my director of operations, also conservative with numbers, build out some of the areas for a real budget—not the pretty, perfect one. The client was furious and assumed the broker lied to him—but in reality, our client had not understood the way these larger property deals run.

Happily, I do deals my way, and while I won't say every deal goes perfectly, because they never do (one of the adventures of real estate investing and property management), I am transparent, and we know to be realistic while still aspiring to strong growth.

> **Property Management Excellence Tip:**
>
> Don't wait until your portfolio becomes too unwieldy before you hire a property manager. You will make a more informed choice if it is not when you are stressed or have a building with critical issues.

## Proptech and the Future

One of the great gifts that the visionary leader, Mike Lansing, from the Boys & Girls Club I belonged to was responsible for was making sure the kids there got to work with real computers and programs and learn technology skills applicable to the real world. Since an early age, I've been very into technology. Once I got into property management, I saw the potential—and I have tried to stay very future-facing when it comes to how we use technology at Coastline.

Property technology, or "proptech," has seen significant advances in recent years, driven by innovations in digital technology, data analytics, and automation. These advances are transforming how real estate is bought, sold, managed, and occupied. Developments include:

- **Smart building technology:** Internet of Things (IoT) devices are increasingly used in buildings to monitor and control various systems, such as HVAC, lighting, and security. These devices can optimize energy efficiency, enhance security, and improve tenant comfort. Smart systems can automatically adjust environmental controls based on occupancy, weather conditions, or user preferences, reducing operational costs and energy usage.

- **Property management automation:** Software platforms are increasingly automating tasks like rent collection, maintenance requests, lease management, and communication with tenants, reducing the workload for property managers. We have a same-day response policy—and automation and AI will increasingly allow for faster response times.

- **Sustainability and green tech:** I think this will be increasingly important. Advanced energy management systems use AI and IoT to optimize energy usage, reduce waste, and increase the sustainability of buildings. Companies are developing and promoting the use of sustainable materials, such as recycled or renewable resources, to reduce the environmental impact of construction.

- **Tenant experience platforms:** Mobile apps and platforms are being developed to enhance the tenant experience, offering features like easy communication with property managers.

- **Security and access control:** Buildings are increasingly using biometric systems, such as fingerprint or facial recognition, for secure and convenient access control. Advanced security systems with AI capabilities offer remote monitoring and real-time alerts, enhancing safety in residential and commercial properties.

These advances in proptech are reshaping the real estate industry, making it more efficient, transparent, and responsive to the needs of tenants, property owners, and investors. For me, it's an exciting time to see where this technology can take our industry—and how it can further improve our processes. As you consider adopting technology, consider your specific niche and business and what tools can help you manage them in the most efficient way possible. That's what technology is supposed to do—improve our efficiencies.

# Growing Our People

There is no property management excellence without excellent people. When you hire employees with a purpose, who are fulfilled, they bring energy and dedication to every interaction, enriching relationships with tenants, clients, and their colleagues. Everyone thinks they hire the best, but we think we *really* do, because as a company we can attract the best because of how we treat our team, how we value them, and how we want them to grow along with us. Whether that is supporting their charities by matching their giving, or paying for them to obtain new training, we show we care about them as people.

But it was a journey to get here.

A few years ago, as I mentioned earlier, Lauren and I were driving up the coast, and she was reading the book *The Dream Manager* by Matthew Kelly. In a nutshell, the book is a parable of a fictional company that is struggling. It comes up with a radical new way to lead by helping employees achieve their own personal dreams.[5] This in turn inspires passion and loyalty for the company—and life itself. Lauren was so excited reading this that she read out passages to me. We were energized by this concept that we wanted to create this type of role in our own company.

Lauren, as a licensed clinical social worker, has an incredible gift for really discerning people, an open heart to try to understand them. When she came on, she wanted to truly discover what motivates our people, what really drives them, what gets them to that next level. She was going to be our own dream manager.

Going back to our theme of listening, Lauren at first really listened to people those first few months. She went and talked to every employee in depth. But they didn't quite get to the "dream" part because what she heard were issues within the company. They ranged from hiring issues, trouble with retention, to leadership having their own concerns. When we really started to listen to the team and what it was that they needed to move forward, and help us grow and help *them* grow, our vision shifted.

When we *really* listened, we discovered they were feeling strain. We needed more people. We were in the midst of coming out of COVID-19, of that Great Resignation, people were burned out. We all—every one of us—had our own struggles and worries during the

---

5    Mazzei et al., "Search for Clues in Miami Collapse."

pandemic. The property management industry and other front-line types of jobs were especially stressful. What we heard from our team is that we needed to be looking for quality people who wanted to be a part of our vision for now and the future. For me, listening in that capacity, I ended up hearing where and what our organizational holes were.

When we had been so excited about the *Dream Manager* book, the concept was really to value the team member and ask, What is that dream? Is it to buy a house? Is it to learn a language? Is it to get to the next level? And then how can we practically make that happen with you?

In addition, as Lauren listened, she also heard that our team members wanted more training here, more support there. Maybe it was coming out of the pandemic, but her discussions with them showed they were actually thinking about the business. They were telling us how we could support them better. We heard it from the top, but then we went through every employee, every team. When we sat down with someone who was explaining a problem—whether it was about a process, a piece of equipment, or a technology—we would ask them to explain the issue clearly so we could understand it from *their* perspective.

I remember saying, "Can you explain to me what the bottleneck is? Why can't this get done so we can help? What specifically can be done to help?" For me, it was important to be in that with them—to understand the grit and the details of their jobs.

Over the years, I had learned some bad leadership habits. Initially, I tended to think like others I'd seen who moved people like chess pieces a bit. The chess master is making all the decisions in that case. I can become too focused on processes and efficiencies and not enough on leading with intention (though Lauren will elbow me when I fall back into old habits). Lauren, through her approach, helped me shift my mindset. She viewed Coastline Equity as her social work client, carefully studying each person's role to ensure they had what they needed to thrive.

For example, understanding people as she did, when she, in a human resources capacity, would look through résumés and narrow down candidates, she carefully considered the supervisor she would be placing a candidate with. She wanted a "match" so they could seamlessly support each other.

Understanding what made each supervisor tick meant she would know which candidate would be a successful match. It started becoming more of a puzzle piece and seeing where each person could contribute best to our company—and where they would be happiest. We also listened more carefully to the skill sets, technology background, and other desired traits that supervisors told us would lead to more success for that new hire.

With this approach, hiring and retention problems were alleviated. In fact, in order to avoid employment issues like all companies faced during the pandemic, we probably have overhired. We found the very best, most terrific matches for our team, and now we have a very deep bench.

However, we haven't ignored the lessons of *The Dream Manager*, even though we adjusted it a bit. Once someone comes aboard, we still want to understand what makes that person tick. We want to know what motivates them. What is their driver?

You might think of it a bit like *The Five Love Languages* by Gary Chapman—but for business. If you are unfamiliar with the five languages, he writes that there are five distinct ways people give and receive love: Words of Affirmation, Acts of Service, Receiving

Gifts, Quality Time, and Physical Touch.[6] Each person tends to have one or two primary love languages that make them feel most loved and appreciated.

Words of Affirmation involve verbal expressions of appreciation, while Acts of Service show love through helpful actions. Receiving Gifts focuses on thoughtful presents, Quality Time emphasizes undivided attention, and Physical Touch conveys affection through physical closeness.[7] Understanding these love languages can improve relationships by fostering more meaningful connections.

Applying that to work, some people just need that "Great job!" They need that personal recognition. Some people need ten minutes of your time in the week. Someone else might like a handwritten note of recognition. Another wants that award at the annual dinner (whereas someone else might be mortified to be called up in front of everyone). Even something as simple as a coffee gift card, or a chocolate left on a desk—a gesture that says, "You matter"—is a driver for why they like to work for you.

We also try to help our team maintain a growth mindset. I recognize that some people are happy in the positions that they're in. They work nine-to-five and are happy to head home to their families and leave their work issues behind. They don't want additional stress. They are content. That is wonderful.

Others want to go beyond where they are, and while they may like where they are, they are not content—they want to grow. They want to go from assistant property manager to property manager, or from maintenance tech to a more skilled tradesperson. For any professional organization, trainings, or college or community college

---

6     Gary Chapman, *The Five Love Languages: How to Express Heartfelt Commitment to Your Mate* (Northfield Publishing, 1995), 23.

7     Chapman, *The Five Love Languages*.

classes, like blueprint reading or trade studies, we reimburse them 100 percent after they finish the coursework and any certifications. If they want to go get their real estate license, we reimburse the entire coursework and all the tests.

Lauren, in particular, spent time asking the personal questions about what drives each employee. And I would be remiss if I did not share that I grew through all this too. I learned my own blind spots, and I learned to be a better listener. Lauren's process helped us all grow. To be a future-facing property management company, it is important to look beyond the immediate work orders and daily tasks to grow not just your portfolio and company—but your people as well.

# CHAPTER 7

## Quality of Life

*Property Management Excellence and Its Impact*

---

**Quality is never an accident; it is always the result of intelligent effort.**
—JOHN RUSKIN

---

Property management has provided me and Lauren—and Coastline Equity itself—with incredible opportunities. We also have a holistic understanding that property management affects quality of life—for tenants, property owners, property managers, and the community itself. For example, think of properties that have fallen into disrepair. Residents' quality of life is impacted. In the case of a commercial tenant, a property that has been neglected will not entice people to work, shop, or visit the businesses there.

## PROPERTY MANAGEMENT EXCELLENCE

Owning investment properties can be lucrative, offering a steady income stream (and as we will see in the "Legacy" chapter, often as a generational asset) and potential long-term appreciation in value. However, managing these properties brings a unique set of challenges that can impact the quality of life for property owners and investors, as well as tenants. Balancing financial goals with the demands of property management, tenant relationships, and personal well-being requires careful planning and foresight. Real estate investing and property management are long-term games. It's a marathon, not a sprint. It's about making smart decisions today that will pay off tomorrow, and when done right, those payoffs can lift entire communities.

Before we go on, we should probably define *quality of life*. Every year, cities and towns are evaluated all over the United States (and the world) with measurements like the World Happiness Index[8] or quality of life indices.[9] Properties also have a quality of life—a microcosm of a community and what it is like to live there.

A good baseline definition for quality of life, as we'll use it in this book, is that it refers to the general well-being of individuals and communities, encompassing a broad range of factors that contribute to people's happiness, health, comfort, and ability to pursue their goals. It includes physical and mental health, financial stability, personal safety, education, social relationships, environmental quality, and access to services and opportunities that allow for a fulfilling and meaningful life. All right—that's a *lot*. But where you live and work and how those places are managed and cared for are a big part of that.

This definition highlights that quality of life is multidimensional. Property management companies play a critical role in the relation-

---

8   "World Happiness Report," accessed October 3, 2024, https://worldhappiness.report/.

9   "Best Places to Live for Quality of Life," US News & World Report, accessed October 3, 2024, https://realestate.usnews.com/places/rankings/best-places-to-live-for-quality-of-life.

ship between tenants and investors (property owners). Quality-of-life issues in our context also refer to the challenges, concerns, and expectations that both tenants and investors face when dealing with property management. It also encompasses our commitment to maintain properties in a way that enhances the lives of the owners/investors as well as the people who work and live there.

In this chapter, I will share the quality of life hierarchies that we use—and they are applicable to the various stakeholders in property management. I hope readers can see how they can use them in their own business or adapt them. But first, let's look at how they all work together to create quality of life (see Figure 7.1).

*Figure 7.1. The Property Management Excellence Quality of Life Ecosystem*

All of the elements of property management excellence, all we have covered in the book until now, have brought us to this point where we can see how they create a dynamic ecosystem.

# Quality of Life for Tenants

Property management might sound as if it is about maintaining a property and buildings—but we do that to provide a positive quality of life for the people who live and work in those buildings. Remember the story of when we took over management of a property where tenants hadn't bothered to turn in work orders—because nothing ever got done? After we waded through all seven hundred or so and set about addressing each and every single one, tenant satisfaction and quality of life grew exponentially.

Much of quality of life as it applies to tenants is addressed in our Renter's Bill of Rights, which we covered in chapter 5. It is why we feel so strongly about the Bill of Rights—and it is a reason I truly urge our industry as a whole to embrace a standard when it comes to tenants' rights. This is property management excellence for our whole industry. We want tenants to know what they can expect from us. All relationships between property owners and tenants amount to a contract that spells out the rights and responsibilities for both. The elements of quality of life for tenants (both commercial and residential) are spelled out in Figure 7.2, in our Quality of Life for Tenants hierarchy.

CHAPTER 7

# QUALITY OF LIFE FOR TENANTS

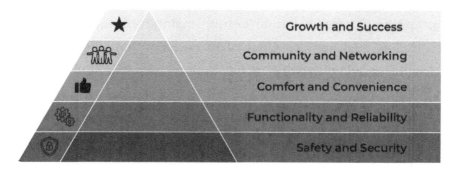

*Figure 7.2. The Property Management Excellence Quality of Life for Tenants Hierarchy*

The foundation of this hierarchy is **safety and security**. The bottom line is if you are in property management and cannot provide safety and security on your properties, there is no baseline for attracting tenants. That is the absolute minimum—the foundation—on which to build upon the other quality of life needs.

Proper security measures, such as functional locks, well-lit common areas, and security cameras, are essential for tenants' peace of mind. Management should address any safety concerns within the community, such as unauthorized access or criminal activity. Safety is something every tenant has a right to demand. I know, from my upbringing, the communities where I felt safe—and the communities where I did not.

The safety and security foundation is not just a well-maintained property, but also the security of clear, proactive communication. Property managers should not wait for problems to arise. Regular check-ins and clear, transparent communication help companies address concerns before the problems become reasons to leave.

## PROPERTY MANAGEMENT EXCELLENCE

Above safety and security is the next level—**functionality and reliability**. In residential properties, amenities like gyms, pools, or communal spaces should be well maintained and accessible. Common areas are also essential in terms of maintenance. The cleanliness and upkeep of areas like hallways, elevators, and parking lots contribute to a tenant's overall living experience. In commercial buildings, lobbies and waiting areas should be well maintained and lit, and the cleanliness and general appearance of public spaces should be exemplary.

> **Property Management Excellence Tip:**
>
> Do not underestimate how "little" things—bulbs out or fresh paint needed in common areas, a nonworking elevator, scrubby weeds in landscaping—impact how tenants and potential tenants view your property.

Reliability is enhanced when excellent tenant relationships, excellent proptech, and solid maintenance and preventive measures come into play so this property is indeed a reliable one for its tenants.

Property managers should also establish clear and open channels of communication with tenants—the managers themselves must be reliable. This includes being accessible via phone, email, or in-person meetings, and responding promptly to tenant inquiries or concerns—again, technology can be used, such as to request maintenance. But even with my love of technology, I understand that AI and cool apps are not the keys to property management excellence. They help with efficiencies, but they are not substitutes for relationships.

For commercial tenants, regular, reliable updates about building operations, maintenance schedules, and any changes to the property are essential. For example, if a parking lot is scheduled to be repaved, this will mean people cannot easily shop at a strip mall, and it necessarily is going to affect business for your commercial tenants. Residential tenants also appreciate being informed about upcoming events, repairs, or policy changes.

Next on our hierarchy comes **comfort and convenience**—as a property manager, you need to put yourself in the shoes of your tenants. Delays in addressing maintenance requests can significantly affect a tenant's quality of life. Issues like plumbing leaks, HVAC failures, or pest infestations require prompt attention.

Much of quality of life as it applies to tenants is addressed in our Renter's Bill of Rights. It is why we feel so strongly about it—and is a reason I truly urge our industry as a whole to embrace a standard when it comes to tenants' rights. We want tenants to know what they can expect from us. All relationships between property owners and tenants amount to a contract that spells out the rights and responsibilities for both. When it comes, though, to where people work and live, the significant issues regarding quality of life focus around the following:

**Maintenance and repairs.** Delays in addressing maintenance requests can significantly affect a tenant's quality of life. Issues like plumbing leaks, HVAC failures, or pest infestations require prompt attention. Even HVAC issues like a building being too hot or too cold can create an uncomfortable environment.

For commercial tenants, quality of life in the workplace is crucial. A comfortable, well-maintained, and functional workspace contributes to employee productivity, job satisfaction, and overall business success. Here I am in property management as a career, and I practically need a parka when I work in our rented office space. This is a chronic issue, day after day, and regular maintenance requests do not fix it (HVAC is a notoriously difficult problem to solve—but I shouldn't need to bring mittens in July). I can also attest that working day after day in a place where basic comfort—such as temperature—is not handled affects my feelings toward my workplace.

When it comes right down to it, I think all property management companies must ask themselves a personal question. Would I let my mother/child/friend live or work here? If the answer is no, action must be taken immediately with the strongest sense of urgency. Dignity and respect for all are hallmarks of quality of life.

**Communication.** I learned firsthand as a leader that a lack of communication could upset the delicate ecosystem of a company. I think as a leader, it's not possible to overcommunicate. It is why I have tried to leverage tech to communicate with my team. When it comes to relationships with tenants, too, they also have a right to expect property management companies to be easily reachable for any issues or concerns.

# CHAPTER 7

> **Property Management Excellence Tip:**
>
> The Rule of Seven in communication and marketing is the concept that people need to hear or see a message at least seven times before they take action or retain the information. This principle is based on the idea that repetition increases the likelihood of a message sticking in someone's mind and influencing their decisions, including memory reinforcement, overcoming distractions, building trust, and message consistency. People are more likely to remember a message when it is repeated multiple times. Repetition helps reinforce the message and make it more familiar, increasing the chances that the audience will retain it.
>
> In practice, the "Rule of Seven" doesn't mean you repeat the exact same phrase or content seven times. Rather, it suggests that the core message should be communicated through multiple channels and forms: calls, emails, newsletters, social media, video, etc.

Lack of effective communication can lead to misunderstandings and unresolved issues. Clear communication about rent increases, policy changes, or community issues is crucial. Unexpected changes can create stress for tenants. In the end, property management is about relationship building—not just ensuring a leaky pipe is fixed—and relationships are based on communication. Again, leveraging technology to aid in timely responses is a key.

**Tenant retention programs.** Offering incentives such as discounted rent for early renewals can encourage tenants to stay longer. This is particularly important in competitive markets where tenants have many options. Implementing a loyalty program for long-term tenants can enhance tenant satisfaction and retention. Feeling valued contributes to quality of life.

**Providing value-added services.** One aspect of quality of life revolves around value-added services. For residential properties, offering convenience services like package handling, laundry services, or cleaning can significantly enhance the tenant experience. For commercial properties, offering additional services such as mail handling, conference room access, or tech support can add value to the tenancy. In large buildings, for example, in this era of everyone ordering just about everything online, package handling alone can be a massive added service. This can be achieved using automated mail systems or by including it as a part of the on-site property manager's duties.

**Energy efficiency and sustainability initiatives.** I live in one of the cities where we manage properties—and I want to be part of a sustainable community where quality of life is considered for all our neighbors. Implementing energy-efficient practices and sustainability initiatives can appeal to environmentally conscious tenants. This might include recycling programs, energy-efficient appliances, or LEED certification for commercial properties. These initiatives can also positively impact net operating income (NOI) through energy/cost savings.

Quality of life isn't just a vague concept—it's a tangible aspect of property management that directly impacts the comfort, satisfaction, and well-being of your tenants. Whether they are living in residential units or working in commercial spaces, their environment influences their daily experience. When tenants feel valued and comfortable, it leads to increased productivity, higher satisfaction, and a deeper sense of well-being. But beyond these benefits, creating a high quality of life plays a large role in tenant retention and lease renewals—key drivers of consistent cash flow and long-term property success.

Next in our hierarchy is **community and networking.** Whether that is creating a sense of community in a large residential property or a retail shopping center, it is the property manager who can set the tone of the community.

Both commercial and residential tenants value community and networking for different yet overlapping reasons, which center on enhancing their experiences, creating opportunities, and fostering a sense of belonging. For commercial tenants, this can mean business opportunities, shared resources (for example, businesses that feel a sense of community may choose to market or advertise together to share costs). In addition, a strong sense of community can make the area more attractive to customers and clients, offering them a better, more cohesive experience (e.g., themed events or marketplaces).

Building a sense of community within a residential property can significantly enhance tenant satisfaction and retention. People often want to feel connected to their neighbors, fostering trust and making the place feel like home. A tight-knit community can enhance a feeling of safety. Knowing your neighbors can create an informal support network where people look out for each other. Tenants who feel part of a community are more likely to stay longer, reducing vacancy rates and turnover for property owners.

Finally, when all of the levels of the hierarchy are fulfilled, we reach the pinnacle. There is growth and success—for the tenant (such as in a commercial space) and for the property management company itself. As someone who's deeply invested in building thriving communities, I know that keeping tenants happy and renewing their leases isn't just good business—it's essential for long-term success. Losing a tenant isn't just a vacancy; it's a ripple effect of costs and challenges that can significantly impact your investment.

When a tenant chooses not to renew their lease, the immediate concern is often the loss of rental income. But that is a shortsighted reaction. The true cost of losing a tenant reaches far deeper.

First, of course, there is the loss of income. In a large commercial space, say, ten thousand feet, regardless of the cost per square foot, the loss will be felt in the investor's bottom line. Then there is the cost of attracting a new tenant. While real estate commissions and regulations are, as of the writing, in a state of flux, commissions are part of the cost of leasing to a new tenant. New tenants often expect improvements to the space (called tenant improvement or TI allowances)—whether it's new flooring, updated fixtures, or a complete remodel. Renewing leases generally have more modest allowances or no costs at all.

> **Property Management Excellence Tip:**
>
> **The true cost of tenant turnover is not just a vacant property. The costs of that vacancy can ripple through your portfolio. Building trust and relationships with tenants is part of the owner mindset.**

When you add up all these factors—vacancy loss, marketing costs, commissions, and TI allowances—the cost of losing a tenant can easily exceed half a million dollars in commercial leasing and property management.[10] This figure doesn't even account for the potential loss of momentum in your building's community or the impact on overall tenant satisfaction. For example, losing an anchor

---

10  Phil Mobley, "The Importance of Tenant Retention and the True Cost of Losing a Tenant," Building Engines, August 15, 2018, https://www.buildingengines.com/blog/true-cost-of-losing-a-tenant/.

store or business that draws traffic to a commercial building can cause other businesses to lose money, or to be unhappy with an "abandoned-looking" property.

In fact, according to the white paper *The Economic Cost of Losing a Tenant*, the cost of losing and subsequently acquiring a replacement tenant can cost building owners up to three times more than renewing a lease.[11]

So how do you avoid these costs? It's simple: focus on tenant retention—which is based on the hierarchy. When tenants feel valued and heard, they're more likely to stay. We actively seek feedback from our tenants to understand what they need and how we can improve—and we like to know when our people are doing great things too. This ongoing dialogue ensures we're always aligned with their expectations.

Actively listening to tenant concerns and suggestions is key to building trust. Property managers should regularly solicit feedback through surveys or informal conversations and show that tenant input is valued by taking appropriate actions. Once again, "same-day response" and quickly addressing tenant concerns go a very long way—when tenants are happy with their quality of life, investors can be too! Tenant retention is about more than just avoiding vacancies—it's about building a community where people want to stay. By focusing on delivering exceptional service, maintaining open lines of communication, and continually improving the tenant experience, you can reduce turnover and protect your investment from the high costs of losing a tenant.

---

11   JLL, "Trends and Insights," accessed October 4, 2024, https://www.us.jll.com/en/trends-and-insights?utm_source=website&utm_medium=whitepaper&utm_campaign=propertymanagement.

Conducting regular tenant satisfaction surveys allows property managers to gather feedback on what is working well and what could be improved. This proactive approach can help identify potential issues before they become significant problems. It can be as simple as a little two-question survey: Was your repair request handled within the time promised? Did the person handling your request deliver superior customer service? But gathering this feedback can provide the astute property manager with valuable insights.

The hierarchy peaks with success and positive growth and a quality of life that tenants can feel positive about.

# Quality of Life for Property Owners

Next, we will explore the quality of life for property owners. The foundation for property owners (see Figure 7.3) in our hierarchy is **financial security**. Whether this is an inherited property, someone is investing in a syndication deal, or they are actively expanding their portfolio, financial security at the foundation.

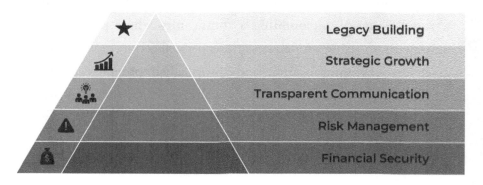

*Figure 7.3. The Property Management Excellence Hierarchy for Property Owners and Investors*

# CHAPTER 7

I have seen many times how one generation may have a real estate portfolio as a pathway to financial freedom. They may find a passion there. But that does not mean the next generation wants to step into a property management role. For this kind of property owner, having a property management company makes total sense. They can reap the intended financial benefits of their inheritance without also inheriting all of the complexities of property management (including the fact that it can be a twenty-four-seven job at times). If the decision is made to hire a company to manage a real estate portfolio, then hopefully the concepts and principles in this book can help an investor formulate questions to ask prospective companies.

The next level up is **risk management**. As I wrote in the previous chapter, growth and success are different for every property owner and investor. Even the story of Coastline has that element. George was looking to derisk his portfolio—and I was young and hungry and willing to take on more risk (within reason!). As a real estate investor, managing risk is crucial to protecting your investment and ensuring long-term profitability. Property managers play a key role in helping investors mitigate various risks associated with real estate ownership and operation.

These areas include tenant screening / lease management, ensuring employment verification, rental history, and credit checks are completed. Maintenance and prompt repairs not only are important to attract and retain tenants, but they are also essential to risk management. Slips and falls or other injuries can occur because of neglectful property management.

The decision of whether to keep managing properties yourself or to hire an outside firm is often made at a tipping point. As I keep saying, property managers are paid to handle problems. Important to that is **transparent communication**. As I wrote earlier in the book, sometimes property owners are surprised to discover our statements are so detailed, and we show the bids we received on various projects, etc. This sort of transparency should be the norm in our industry. For investors' quality of life and the concerns close to them, transparency and accurate financial accounting are absolutely essential (and this is not always followed by our industry—and is something I really am rallying for). Property managers should provide detailed and accurate financial reports that track income, expenses, and cash flow. Regular reporting helps investors monitor the financial health of their investments and make informed decisions to manage cash flow risks.

Investors should also receive regular updates on key performance indicators (KPIs) related to the property, such as occupancy rates, rent collection rates, tenant turnover, and lease renewals. These updates help investors stay informed about the property's operational performance.

When selecting vendors for property maintenance, repairs, or other services, property managers should be transparent about the selection process, the costs involved, and any relationships they may have with the vendors. This prevents conflicts of interest and ensures that vendors are chosen based on quality and cost-effectiveness.

Next, we have **strategic growth**—that looks different for every property owner. Coastline has its own vision for strategic growth for ourselves as well. There is no one-size-fits-all approach in property management.

When all these aspects of the hierarchy are working in conjunction, then you have true **legacy building**—the peak of this hierarchy. A real estate portfolio is a wonderful legacy investment and often a multigenerational asset. We will discuss this in greater detail in the next chapter.

Finally, before we move on, one big quality of life question that self-managing property owners often face is that from a property management perspective, every investor will face a moment, as their portfolio grows, when they must decide if they will continue managing their properties themselves or hire a property management company. (Maybe that's even why you bought this book.) For some, investing in real estate starts as a side hustle, and then it grows until it's a full-time job and then some. In fact, there is often real "relief" when someone whose portfolio is now overwhelming them gets to hand over the reins. Another common quality-of-life scenario in the inherited real estate portfolio.

When looking at quality of life from that investor's perspective, it helps to keep the following in mind:

# Return on Investment (ROI)

High occupancy rates are critical for maximizing rental income. Investors expect property management companies to effectively market properties and attract reliable tenants. Quality of life for tenants ultimately means a better ROI for investors.

When it comes to rent collection, it should be timely and efficient—ideally using new tech to maximize those efficiencies for everyone involved. Anything property managers can do to streamline processes for tenants and their team will pay off on the bottom line.

# Property Maintenance

One of the issues I have found with investors and cash flow is an underestimation of what is involved with property maintenance. It is a delicate balancing act between careful stewardship of finances and proactive maintenance. Obviously, unexpected expenses can impact profitability. Too often, property managers, syndicators, or investors will paint a rosy picture of maintenance and cash flow. However, as I mentioned in an earlier chapter, I am one of those business leaders who hopes for the best, plans for the worst—but always has a plan. As an investor, you should plan for potential repairs and maintenance, and building that into your budget and forecasting will offer peace of mind.

# Risk Management

As a real estate investor, managing risk is crucial to protecting your investment and ensuring long-term profitability. Property managers play a key role in helping investors mitigate various risks associated with real estate ownership and operation. These areas include tenant screening / lease management, ensuring employment verification, rental history, and credit checks are completed. Maintenance and prompt repairs not only are important to attract and retain tenants, but they are also essential to risk management. Slips and falls or other injuries can occur because of neglectful property management.

In addition, property managers must be well versed in local, state, and federal laws that govern real estate ownership and operations. They must ensure that the property complies with all regulations, including fair housing laws, health and safety codes, and tenant rights. Compliance reduces the risk of fines, penalties, and legal disputes. This is another reason those who inherit real estate portfolios will often hire property management companies. The heirs may not be remotely familiar with all the legal risk and compliance issues—and may not even live in the same city or state!

CHAPTER 7

# Transparency and Accurate Financial Reporting

As I mentioned, cash flow and expenses related to property management are sometimes a surprise for new investors who only pictured large profits without realizing all of the other pieces of property management and investing. For investors' quality of life and the concerns close to them, transparency and accurate financial accounting are absolutely essential (and this is not always followed by our industry—and is something I am really rallying for). Property managers should provide detailed, timely, and accurate financial reports that track income, expenses, and cash flow. Regular reporting helps investors monitor the financial health of their investments and make informed decisions to manage cash flow risks.

Investors should also receive regular updates on key performance indicators (KPIs) related to the property, such as occupancy rates, rent collection rates, tenant turnover, and lease renewals. These updates help investors stay informed about the property's operational performance.

When selecting vendors for property maintenance, repairs, or other services, property managers should be transparent about the selection process, the costs involved, and any relationships they may have with the vendors. This prevents conflicts of interest and ensures that vendors are chosen based on quality and cost-effectiveness.

# Tenant Relations and Communication

Strong tenant relations are essential for reducing turnover rates and maintaining a stable rental income. Property managers must foster good relationships with tenants through regular communication, prompt responses to concerns, and by ensuring that the property is well maintained. When there are problems—and there always will be—for an investor's own peace of mind, not taking it personally is important. We train our property managers in how to cool down a conversation that's getting into the "Red Zone" of anger. Now, in fact, we'll discuss the people essential to our company—quality of life for property managers.

## Quality of Life for Property Managers

There are so many different directions that property management can pull people. As a property management company, we have whole teams to help us manage our portfolio—and we still need to ensure that our property managers find balance in their lives. For owners who self-manage their portfolios, it can get very overwhelming, particularly if you do not have a background in property management. Here are some of the big challenges property owners and managers face that impact their quality of life (Figure 7.4).

**QUALITY OF LIFE FOR PROPERTY MANAGERS**

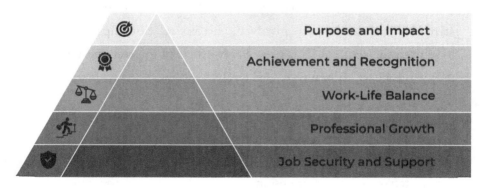

*Figure 7.4. Property Management Excellence Hierarchy for Quality of Life for Property Managers*

Here, our foundation is **job security and support**—which is why Lauren was such a huge help to us with her approach to human resources. We feel that developing our people—paying for further certifications, for example, or learning the way in which they like to receive feedback or positive affirmations—demonstrates to them the support they have.

**Professional growth** is not only about paying for certifications, but also promoting from within, and "growing" the people who want to go far in property management and investing. We love to attract employees who have sky's-the-limit energy and ambition—and then support them as they set their own professional goals.

Next, one of the most significant issues affecting the quality of life for property owners and managers is **work-life balance**, including time management. Investment properties, especially those with multiple units or located in different locations, require a substantial time commitment. In Southern California, where traffic is one of Dante's Circles of Hell, just getting between properties can take time. Tasks such as responding to tenant inquiries, handling maintenance requests, conducting property inspections, and managing financial records can be time-consuming and overwhelming.

On our team, we have recently been working with different time management models. Because a property manager's "to-do" list is normally a frightening compendium of too many things to possibly accomplish in a single day, we work with our team to identify the core "to-do" items that are essential for the portfolio and to move that portfolio and the obligations toward it forward. After core tasks are accomplished, the many other tasks can be delegated, handled, and checked off. (See Figure 7.5.)

To mitigate the real challenges of time management, many property owners turn to professional property management services.

## PROPERTY MANAGEMENT EXCELLENCE

While this can alleviate some of the time pressures, it also introduces another layer of oversight, as owners must ensure that the management company is performing its duties effectively. Choosing a reputable management company and establishing clear communication and expectations are crucial steps in preserving time for other important areas of life.

> **Property Management Excellence Tip:**
>
> Do not wait until you are completely burned out and overextended to look into efficiencies and time management approaches that can help you manage your properties or to begin interviewing property management companies.

# CHAPTER 7

# TO-DO LIST

**DATE**

### TOP 3 PRIORITIES

- ☐ ..........................
- ☐ ..........................
- ☐ ..........................

### NOTES

### TO-DO

- ☐ ..........................
- ☐ ..........................
- ☐ ..........................
- ☐ ..........................
- ☐ ..........................
- ☐ ..........................
- ☐ ..........................
- ☐ ..........................
- ☐ ..........................
- ☐ ..........................
- ☐ ..........................
- ☐ ..........................
- ☐ ..........................
- ☐ ..........................
- ☐ ..........................
- ☐ ..........................
- ☐ ..........................
- ☐ ..........................
- ☐ ..........................
- ☐ ..........................

### DAILY ACTIVITIES LIST

1. Emergencies
2. AppFolio Dashboard
   A. Work orders
   B. Delinquencies
   C. Overdue activities
   D. Move ins and Move out
3. Voicemails
4. E-Mails
5. Work Orders
6. Bills
7. Credit Card Receipts
8. Work Order Labor Summary
9. To-Do List
10. Calendar
11. Inspections

Before the end of your day, it's key that you respond to all phone calls, text messages, and emails that came in during today's business hours.

*Figure 7.5. Property Management Excellence To-Do Time Management List*

## PROPERTY MANAGEMENT EXCELLENCE

We have discussed tenant relations, but for the property manager, this can be a source of tremendous stress. Sometimes I think I almost try to talk people *out* of going into property management. I make sure they understand that it means dealing with problems every day. While that makes for an unpredictable day that some may love, for those sensitive to criticism or who do not like having to manage and support an unhappy tenant (or a nonpaying one, for that matter), this might not be the field for you.

For us, we have the Equity Approach (seen earlier in chapter 4)—it guides relationships with our tenants and teams. And it is nonnegotiable.

Challenges in tenant relations can arise from various sources. Tenants may have unreasonable demands, fail to pay rent on time, or cause damage to the property. On the flip side, the property management may be unsatisfactory, maintenance requests delayed or ignored, and more. Our Renter's Bill of Rights sets out the expectations in both directions (which, again, is why I would like to see our industry set a standard).

The cumulative effect of time pressures, tenant relations, and the day-to-day pressures of managing a portfolio can take a toll on the personal well-being of property owners and property managers. The stress of managing investment properties can lead to anxiety, sleep disturbances, and even physical health problems. It can also strain relationships with family and friends, as the demands of property management can consume time and energy that might otherwise be spent on personal connections and self-care.

Remember my story about Lauren and me having to leave Disneyland shortly after we got there, as we anticipated issues related to a sudden heavy rain? For one thing, Lauren was "in it" with me, as far as property management. She understood. For another, we are season-pass people (we're Disney superfans—yes, some would call us the infamous Disney adults!)—so we knew we could come back. Even the next day if we wanted.

But now picture that *same* story if we had saved up for a couple of months or even years for this big, fun weekend at Disney, and we needed to turn around and go home. So you can imagine a property manager facing the same thing while his or her kids are looking at them (another reason I tell our property managers to screen calls on weekends, nights, and holidays—not everything is an emergency).

Another tool we offer is seen in Figure 7.6, and it helps our managers with the intense influx of email. It's a system that gives our tenants a same-day response—but also addresses the stress of a busy property manager's inbox.

*Figure 7.6. The Property Management Excellence Inbox Approach*

Inboxes and work "crises" are just part of the day-to-day pressures of life as a property manager. Maintaining a healthy work-life balance is essential for preserving quality of life as a manager. This may involve setting boundaries around the time spent on property management tasks, delegating responsibilities to others, and prioritizing self-care activities such as exercise, relaxation, and socializing. Seeking support from other property owners, joining real estate investment groups, or working with a mentor can also provide valuable insights and reduce feelings of isolation. I know my years spent with George, picking his brain about anything and everything his years in property management had taught him, were invaluable.

Over time, I have developed my own approach for work-life balance as a property manager and CEO. I will be the first to confess I had to learn this the hard way. But here are some practicable suggestions.

**Tips for Maintaining Work-Life Balance:**

- **Set clear boundaries:** Create specific times of the day when you are "off the clock" and stick to them. Not every call or issue requires an immediate response. Save those moments for the real emergencies—they will come.

- **Delegate tasks:** Trust your team to handle routine responsibilities. Delegating not only reduces your workload but also empowers your team to grow.

- **Prioritize self-care:** Make time for activities that help you recharge, whether it's exercise, meditation, or hobbies that bring you joy.

- **Connect with others:** Seek support from other property managers or join real estate groups. Sharing challenges and advice with peers can reduce feelings of isolation.

- **Screen calls and emails:** Develop a system for identifying true emergencies so that nonurgent matters don't interrupt personal time or delay the most important core to-dos.

- **Be present with friends and family:** When spending time with loved ones, try to be fully present.

Over time, Lauren and I developed strategies to manage the constant demands of property management while still making space for our personal lives. Setting boundaries was a big part of that—learning when to delegate, when to turn off work notifications, and how to carve out time for the things that refresh us. It's not always easy, but it's necessary for long-term success.

The next level of this hierarchy is **achievement and recognition**. This, again, is where we see the five love languages at use in our business model.

The peak—**purpose and impact**. As a property manager, each day I am filled with purpose—for my investors, my team, my community.

# Quality of Life for the Community

Property ownership isn't just about managing your investments—it's also about shaping the communities where people live and work. Every decision an owner makes, from setting rent levels to choosing which tenants to accept, ripples through the broader community. When these decisions prioritize profit at the expense of building maintenance or tenant well-being or neglect the needs of the neighborhood, they can fuel issues like displacement, blight, and housing insecurity.

But property ownership also offers a powerful opportunity to do good. Owners who take a socially responsible approach can help strengthen and improve their communities while still generating consistent returns on their investments. This might involve maintaining properties to a higher standard, offering mixed-income housing, or engaging in local initiatives that support local economic development, safety, and neighborhood vitality. These actions not only create a better quality of life for tenants but also foster stability and pride in the community, which in turn benefits the property itself.

Decisions around tenant selection, property improvements, and even partnerships with local businesses can all be made with an eye toward creating positive outcomes for everyone involved (see Figure 7.7).

## QUALITY OF LIFE FOR THE COMMUNITY

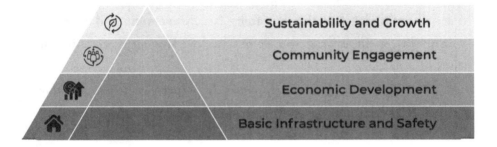

*Figure 7.7. Property Management Excellence Quality of Life for the Community*

Here, of course, the community's foundation is **safety and a solid infrastructure**. Without safe roads, or safe communities, quality of life cannot flourish.

Next is **economic development**. I love seeing other partners in the community, other entrepreneurs, other businesses, and so on, who deeply invest in the world around them. For thriving economic development, there needs to be the next level of the hierarchy—**community engagement**. This can have many facets, from investment in the local economy, partnerships with local organizations, and

# CHAPTER 7

open communication between the property management company and the community itself.

Finally, the peak of this hierarchy is sustainable development and growth. That is when you know the community you are developing is a healthy one.

***

Quality-of-life issues in the context of rental properties affect tenants, investors, property managers, and communities differently, yet these issues are interconnected (recall the Property Management Ecosystem at the beginning of the chapter). Consider your own community and how you can align all the stakeholders.

# CHAPTER 8

## Building a Legacy

*Property Investing for Financial Freedom*

---

**Someone is sitting in the shade today because someone planted a tree a long time ago.**
—WARREN BUFFETT

---

Real estate investing tends to be favored by people wanting to leave a legacy and build generational wealth. While it is not the only way to build wealth or financial freedom, it offers unique opportunities that other investments simply cannot.

I have had investors and clients who have been very clear that they worked hard to build their fortunes, ensuring that they're leaving a healthy real estate portfolio will ensure the next generation is cared for—and the one after that. I've witnessed families manage real estate portfolios over generations, steering their real estate legacies with care. But success is not guaranteed.

There's a well-known statistic, based on a twenty-year study, that followed generational wealth and discovered that 70 percent of families with generational wealth will lose it by the second generation, and 90 percent will lose it by the third.[12] I have heard a lot of more emotional armchair quarterbacking as to why that is. By the third generation, the kids have grown lazy because they have grown up in wealth. However, that is often not the case. Sometimes it can be the case of a star or wealthy person who is no longer at the height of their success, spending like they still are.

The reality is it can happen for several reasons. Businesses may fail to adapt to a changing world. Technology renders old business models obsolete (remember one-hour photo shops?). Or sometimes a portfolio is simply not balanced and flexible enough to weather economic storms.

This is why a stable, well-diversified real estate portfolio is essential to building a lasting legacy. But there's more to legacy than dollars. To me, legacy means passing down values like integrity, hard work, and community involvement, alongside financial assets. These values are the true bedrock that allows future generations to thrive.

Now let's examine why real estate investing tends to be a legacy investment. Real estate's unique ability to generate steady income, appreciate in value, and offer tax benefits makes it a powerful tool for creating financial security and a lasting legacy.

- **Steady income generation:** One of the most attractive benefits of owning a real estate portfolio is the cash flow it can generate

---

12   Lee Kong Chian School of Business, "How to Beat the Third-Generation Curse," Singapore Management University, 2024, https://business.smu.edu.sg/master-wealth-management/lkcsb-community/how-beat-third-generation-curse.

through rental payments (which is why tenant retention is so important). Unlike other investments that might be more volatile or dependent on market timing, rental properties can provide consistent cash flow, making it easier to cover expenses, reinvest in additional properties, or build wealth over time.

Steady income is essential for legacy building because it ensures financial stability across generations. It allows for continued investment and growth while providing for family needs. For example, many people start small—buying a triplex and living in one unit while renting out the other two. This creates both income and equity, which can be used to expand their portfolio.

- **Appreciation in property value:** Real estate tends to appreciate in value over time, especially in areas with growing populations and strong economic conditions. While there may be fluctuations in the real estate market, the general trend is that property values increase over the long term. This appreciation can significantly enhance the value of a real estate portfolio, providing a substantial financial asset that can be passed down to heirs.

  Additionally, the appreciation of properties can increase the equity that owners have in their investments, which can be leveraged for further investment opportunities. Generally, developing a real estate portfolio is a long game, so real estate fluctuations can be absorbed over the life of the property.

- **Tax benefits:** Obviously, every investor's financial picture will be different, but investing in real estate often carries with it tax benefits. For families wanting to leave a legacy, the tax benefits can help heirs keep more of their intended inheritance.

Tax advantages include, for example, property owners being able to deduct expenses related to property management, maintenance, and mortgage interest from their taxable income. Depreciation is another significant tax benefit, allowing owners to reduce their taxable income by accounting for the wear and tear on their properties over time (commercial properties can take depreciation for longer than residential properties). When properties are passed down to heirs, again, depending on how the portfolio was structured, tax advantages can include reducing capital gains taxes on future sales. These tax advantages can help maximize the financial benefits of a real estate portfolio over the long term.

- **Inflation hedge:** Real estate investments are often considered an effective hedge against inflation. Again, real estate investing is a long game—which means the investment will ride out the peaks and valleys of inflationary periods. As the cost of living increases, so do rental prices and property values. This means that the income generated from rental properties typically rises in line with inflation. This characteristic makes real estate a reliable long-term investment that can protect against the eroding effects of inflation, ensuring that the legacy retains its value over the years.

- **Control and flexibility:** Real estate provides more control than other investments. As a property owner, you can make decisions about renovations, tenant selection, and property management strategies, tailoring your portfolio to meet your personal goals. This control also extends to how you pass properties down to your heirs—whether through direct ownership, trusts, or estate planning tools.

Owning a real estate portfolio allows you to balance between being hands-on or delegating to property managers, making it a flexible investment strategy for various stages of life.

- **Job creation and economic development:** A key but often overlooked benefit of real estate investment is its contribution to job creation and economic development. Managing a real estate portfolio requires the support of a variety of professionals—contractors, property managers, landscapers, maintenance teams, and more. As an investor, you're not just building wealth for yourself, you're helping to create jobs and support local businesses. By investing in real estate, you directly contribute to the local economy. Whether it's hiring contractors for renovations, leasing agents to help with vacant properties or maintenance crews, your investment generates employment opportunities. These jobs support families and help sustain the community's economy.

  In addition, when you invest in properties—especially in growing or underserved neighborhoods—you become part of the revitalization process. Your investment can attract other businesses, improve infrastructure, and increase property values in the surrounding area, creating a positive ripple effect for the entire community.

***

For investors committed to both financial returns and community impact, real estate offers a unique opportunity to leave behind more than just wealth—it allows you to create lasting economic growth in the areas where you invest.

# Balancing Wealth Building with Social Impact

A legacy isn't just about money and wealth building—it's about the impact you leave on the world. True legacy comes from not just what you accumulate, but how your investments shape and uplift the communities around you. As real estate investors, we hold immense power to influence neighborhoods, local economies, and the quality of life for countless individuals.

The properties you own, manage, and develop don't just generate income—they also provide homes for families, spaces for businesses to thrive, and opportunities for economic development. This is where financial success intersects with social responsibility. A well-planned real estate portfolio can create both personal financial freedom and positive societal impact, ensuring that your legacy benefits not only your heirs, but also the communities that supported your success.

Investing with an eye toward social impact—whether through affordable housing, revitalization of underserved areas, or community-driven development—ensures your portfolio is aligned with values that stand the test of time. The opportunity to shape neighborhoods, provide stability, and improve lives adds immeasurable value to your legacy. Depending on where you live, how you grew up, and what affordable housing is like in your community, you may not realize that affordable housing can be a tremendous legacy investment—not only for your portfolio (where it is a solid approach to risk management), but it also can leave an imprint on your community or the bigger legacy you want to leave.[13]

Affordable housing provides a powerful opportunity for both financial growth and social responsibility. As housing affordability continues to be a major issue in many urban areas, there is a pressing demand for rental units that offer reasonable rents for low- to middle-income families. Investing in affordable housing allows you to meet that demand while building a profitable real estate portfolio.

Lauren and I are passionate about this issue. More importantly, and I will discuss this more in the next chapter, we realize that property managers absolutely need to be part of the discussions—with city councils, other nonprofits, community leaders, and developers. Often we are on the front lines of the problem.

Affordable housing is typically defined as housing that costs no more than 30 percent of a household's income.[14] When housing expenses exceed this threshold, families are considered cost-burdened, meaning they have less money available for other essentials like food, healthcare, and education. For the millions of families struggling to meet this standard, affordable housing is not just a matter of convenience; it is a necessity for maintaining a basic standard of living. Without Section 8, as a child, I would have gone without much more.

Most would call this a true "crisis." But if we are to look at the problem as investors and property managers, what are some of the causes of this crisis?

---

13   Center on Budget and Policy Priorities, "Research Shows Housing Vouchers Reduce Hardship and Provide Platform for Long-Term Gains Among Children," Center on Budget and Policy Priorities, 2024, https://www.cbpp.org/research/research-shows-housing-vouchers-reduce-hardship-and-provide-platform-for-long-term-gains.

14   US Department of Housing and Urban Development, "Defining Housing Affordability," PD&R Edge, August 14, 2017, https://www.huduser.gov/portal/pdredge/pdr-edge-featd-article-081417.html.

**Rising housing costs.** In many urban areas, the cost of housing has risen dramatically over the past few decades. This increase is driven by a variety of factors, including population growth and the extensive red tape around building new apartments and keeping up with demand. In cities where demand for housing far outpaces supply, prices for both rental and for-sale properties have surged, making it increasingly difficult for low- and middle-income families to afford a place to live.

**Stagnant wages.** Now there's the other side of the rock and a hard place. While housing costs have been rising, wages for many workers have remained stagnant. The widening gap between income and housing costs means that more people are spending a higher percentage of their income on rent or mortgages, leaving them financially vulnerable. This is especially true for low-wage workers, who often find themselves priced out of the neighborhoods where they work.

**Insufficient affordable housing supply.** Affordable housing is essential (we'll talk about the results of the lack of affordable housing in a moment), yet the supply consistently falls short of demand. The waiting lists to get into affording housing programs, like Section 8, are often incredibly long, leaving families in limbo for years or even decades. This shortage is driven by a combination of factors, including the high cost of land and construction, as well as market incentives that push developers to prioritize building luxury apartments or high-end homes, which generate higher profits.

In many cities, developers focus on projects that target wealthier tenants, while affordable housing remains underbuilt. Compounding this issue, existing affordable units are frequently at risk of being converted to market-rate housing due to rising costs to operate these buildings, further shrinking the availability of affordable homes. This imbalance not only displaces low-income residents but also creates economic segregation, as entire neighborhoods become inaccessible to those who need affordable options the most.

Addressing this supply gap requires a commitment to creating incentives for developers to build affordable units, as well as policies that protect and preserve the existing stock of affordable housing. Without these measures, the crisis will continue to deepen, widening the gap between those who can afford housing and those who cannot.

**Government policy and zoning regulations.** Now, as I said at the beginning of this section, property managers and investors need to be part of the discussions on affordable housing. Otherwise, it will be difficult to effect change within, sometimes, the confines of policy and zoning requirements. Government policies and zoning regulations play a significant role in the affordable housing crisis. In some areas, restrictive zoning laws limit the construction of multi-family housing or require large lot sizes, making it more difficult and expensive to build affordable housing. Additionally, the reduction of federal funding for affordable housing programs over the years has contributed to the shortage of affordable units.

**Gentrification.** Gentrification, the process by which higher-income individuals move into lower-income neighborhoods, often leads to the displacement of long-term residents. As property values and rents increase in gentrifying areas, existing residents may find themselves unable to afford their homes, forcing them to move to less expensive, often less desirable, areas.

As I've previously mentioned, I can remember my first property management job was working for a man with a background with Marriott Hotels. He had an *incredible* eye, able to take distressed properties and envision something new for them. I love transforming properties too. But I am aware that sometimes the results add to the affordable housing crisis as the refinished properties drive up prices.

Mitigating the negative effects of gentrification on low-income communities requires a *commitment* to a combination of policy interventions, community engagement, and equitable development strategies from affordable housing strategies to inclusionary zoning (in which new developments must include a certain percentage of affordable housing units), community land trusts (CLTs) (nonprofit, community-run organizations that own land and maintain long-term affordable housing), and more. Property owners and investors need to be thoughtful in their approach to development.

**"Not in my backyard" ("NIMBY"):** The resistance to multifamily housing, often captured in the NIMBY mindset, is a significant obstacle to solving the housing crisis. While many agree on the importance of multifamily housing, they resist having it built near their homes due to misconceptions about property values or community impact. When managed correctly, affordable and market-rate multifamily housing can fit seamlessly into any neighborhood without negative effects.

NIMBY attitudes delay progress and prevent the construction of much-needed housing. As industry professionals, we need to advocate for affordable housing and educate communities about its benefits. Overcoming NIMBYism is key to ensuring that affordable housing is available and integrated into diverse areas, not just relegated to specific neighborhoods.

The lack of affordable housing has far-reaching consequences for individuals, families, and communities. This crisis is not going away. Increasingly, young people cannot afford to move out, or families are returning to two- and three-generation households. It impacts us all and will continue to. Here is a brief examination of the issues we face by not confronting this crisis head on.

**Increased population of unhoused people.** One of the most visible and tragic consequences of the affordable housing crisis is the rise in homelessness. When people cannot afford housing, they are often forced to live in shelters, on the streets, or in substandard conditions. Homelessness has severe implications for physical and mental health, access to education and employment, and overall well-being.

In many areas, the issue is dire for both the sheer number of unhoused people—and the impact on local businesses, the strain on public resources, and the surrounding community. Since cities fluctuate in policies, etc., I will not single any particular place out—but if we don't address this, there will not be a city that is not impacted. But we have seen on the news and in our news feeds, cities where, especially after the COVID-19 pandemic, vacant downtowns and office buildings, and streets lined with tents. This impacts businesses—and revenues to city coffers.

**Economic inequality.** The affordable housing crisis exacerbates economic inequality by concentrating poverty in certain neighborhoods[15] while pushing low-income residents out of more affluent areas. This segregation by income leads to disparities in access to quality education, healthcare, and employment opportunities, perpetuating cycles of poverty. Again, if not addressed, this is a crisis that will just expand as there are more working poor. Sociologist William Julius Wilson, who wrote *The Truly Disadvantaged* and *When Work Disappears*, has been a key figure in popularizing the discussion of neighborhood effects.

**Impact on health.** The stress of living in unaffordable or unstable housing can have significant health impacts. Cost-burdened families

---

15   Ingrid Gould Ellen and Margery Austin Turner, "Do Neighborhoods Matter and Why?," in John Goering and Judith D. Feins, eds., *Choosing a Better Life? Evaluating the Moving to Opportunity Social Experiment* (Urban Institute Press, 2003), 314–38.

may skimp on food, healthcare, or medications to afford rent, leading to malnutrition, untreated illnesses, and mental health issues. Substandard housing conditions, such as mold or inadequate heating, can also contribute to poor health outcomes. However, well-maintained Section 8 housing mitigates health effects.[16]

**Educational disparities and the opportunity gap.** Mentors and leaders at the Boys & Girls Club taught me how to use a computer, how to DJ, and how to apply to college, and tutored me when I struggled. I know firsthand from my childhood and my friends around me that housing instability can have a profound impact on children's education. Frequent moves and unstable living conditions make it difficult for children to succeed in school and make the lasting relationships necessary to succeed in life. Homeless or highly mobile students are more likely to experience absenteeism, lower academic achievement, and higher dropout rates. Affordable housing, again, mitigates this.[17]

Lauren and I are deeply committed to being part of the solution to the affordable housing crisis. Addressing this critical issue requires a multipronged approach that includes policy reform, innovative housing solutions, and active community engagement. One of the most effective ways to increase affordable housing is through policies that encourage its construction, using incentives like subsidies and tax credits, and by relaxing outdated zoning regulations that make building affordable units difficult. Policies that promote mixed-income developments—where market-rate and affordable units coexist—can also help diversify neighborhoods and increase the overall housing supply.

---

16  Mary K. Cunningham et al., "Section 8 Mobility and Neighborhood Health," Urban Institute, April 1, 2000, https://www.urban.org/research/publication/section-8-mobility-and-neighborhood-health.

17  Cunningham et al., "Section 8 Mobility."

# CHAPTER 8

Reforming restrictive zoning laws that limit the construction of affordable housing is critical. Many of these laws were designed in a different era and no longer meet today's housing needs. Allowing for higher-density developments, reducing minimum lot sizes, and streamlining the approval process for affordable housing projects can make it easier and more cost-effective to build affordable units. Often zoning laws are from another era—when new areas need affordable apartments more than ever before.

In addition to building more units, we need to expand and strengthen rental assistance programs. One of the most significant gaps in our system is the lengthy wait time for affordable housing. I've seen firsthand how a single parent, trying to stabilize their family's housing situation, can be caught in limbo, waiting for relief that seems impossibly far off. Lauren is actively involved with an organization (Harbor Connects) working to bridge this gap by providing intermediate housing options for families, offering an alternative to emergency shelters. Too many people fall through the cracks because the very programs meant to help them are fragmented and hard to navigate, especially when they're already overwhelmed by the stress of their housing situation.

Rental assistance programs, such as housing vouchers, can help low-income families afford housing in the private market. Expanding these programs and ensuring that they are adequately funded can reduce the burden of housing costs for those most in need. In addition, I know firsthand that unscrupulous property managers will tell people they do not accept Section 8—when in fact, by law, they must (in many cities and states).

Addressing the NIMBY phenomenon is another critical piece of the puzzle. Policies like inclusionary zoning require developers to include a certain percentage of affordable units in new developments.

These policies can help ensure that affordable housing is integrated into all neighborhoods—rather than being concentrated in certain areas.

The private sector can play a role in addressing the affordable housing crisis through partnerships with governments and nonprofits. Private developers can be incentivized to build affordable housing through tax credits, grants, and other financial incentives. I truly urge my fellow property management companies and those in our industry to get involved.

Now I want to speak directly to investors. There's a common misconception that affordable housing doesn't belong in a profitable real estate portfolio—that it's somehow a poor investment. This couldn't be further from the truth. In reality, affordable housing properties provide stable, consistent rental income, backed by government guarantees. With the right management approach, these properties can be just as lucrative as market-rate units, while also serving a vital social need. Investing in affordable housing doesn't mean sacrificing returns; it means contributing to the solution and building a portfolio that stands for something greater.

**Stable and guaranteed income.** One of the most significant advantages of affordable housing is the stability of rental income. The programs guarantee that a substantial portion of the rent is paid directly by the government, usually through local public housing authorities. This direct payment reduces the risk of rent defaults, providing landlords with a consistent and reliable income stream. In uncertain economic times, this guarantee can be particularly attractive, as it ensures that landlords will receive a steady cash flow even if tenants face financial difficulties.

This involvement of the government in affordable housing provides an additional layer of security for investors. Since the government pays a portion of the rent, and this payment is often adjusted to reflect the fair market value of the property, landlords are assured of receiving rent that is in line with current market conditions.

**Low vacancy rates.** Residents who utilize affordable housing programs, like Section 8 vouchers, often stay in their rental units for extended periods, leading to lower vacancy rates (below 2 percent)[18] compared to market-rate rentals. This long-term tenancy reduces the costs and efforts associated with tenant turnover, such as cleaning, repairs, and marketing the property to new tenants. Additionally, there is typically high demand for Section 8 housing (too high—we need a higher supply of housing), so landlords often have a steady stream of potential tenants, minimizing the risk of long vacancies and lost income.

Residents utilizing affordable housing programs must meet specific income requirements to qualify for the program, and their rent contributions are capped based on their income levels. As a result, these tenants are often more reliable and committed to staying in their rental units. Moreover, since Section 8 housing is in high demand, tenants are motivated to maintain good standing with the program to retain their housing assistance. This can lead to more responsible tenants who take care of the property and adhere to lease agreements.

**Potential for property appreciation.** Though not a given, investing in affordable housing in the right locations can lead to property appreciation over time. Many of these properties are located in areas that are undergoing revitalization or are in proximity to growing urban centers. As neighborhoods improve and property values rise, investors can benefit from the long-term appreciation of

---

18  Novogradac, "Vacancy Rates at LIHTC Properties Remain Below 2 Percent, Continuing Long-Term Trend," Novogradac, 2024, https://www.novoco.com/notes-from-novogradac/vacancy-rates-at-lihtc-properties-remain-below-2-continuing-long-term-trend.

their assets, while still receiving stable rental income through the Section 8 program.

**Tax incentives.** Investors of affordable housing may qualify for various tax incentives, including deductions for mortgage interest, property taxes, depreciation, and expenses related to property maintenance and management. In some cases, local governments may also offer *additional* tax breaks or incentives for providing affordable housing. These tax benefits can significantly enhance the profitability of affordable housing investments, making them an attractive option for investors looking to maximize their returns.

**Positive social impact.** For those, like me, committed to leaving a legacy in their community, investing in affordable housing allows landlords to contribute to those towns and cities by providing safe, affordable housing to low-income families, the elderly, and disabled individuals. This positive social impact can be rewarding on a personal level and can enhance the reputation of the investor within the community. For socially conscious investors, affordable housing offers the opportunity to make a difference while still achieving financial returns.

**Flexibility in property types.** Affordable housing is not limited to a specific type of property. Investors can choose from single-family homes or entire apartment buildings. This flexibility allows investors to diversify their real estate portfolio and select properties that align with their investment strategy and goals. Whether aiming for long-term appreciation, steady cash flow, or a mix of both, affordable housing can be tailored to meet a variety of investment objectives.

Affordable housing represents a compelling investment opportunity for those looking for stable income, low vacancy rates, and reliable tenants. The government-backed security, coupled with potential tax benefits and property appreciation, makes it an attractive option for both seasoned and new real estate investors. Additionally, the opportunity to make a positive social impact by providing affordable housing further enhances the appeal of these investments. By carefully selecting properties and managing them effectively, investors can build a profitable and socially responsible real estate portfolio with Section 8 housing at its core.

***

Investing in affordable housing is not just about financial returns—it's about leaving a lasting legacy. By providing housing that meets a critical need, investors can build a socially responsible and profitable real estate portfolio that benefits both their bottom line and their community. However, from a purely financial perspective, a well-thought-out real estate portfolio can spread out risk, appreciate in value, provide tax benefits—and be there for your heirs or designated beneficiaries.

# CHAPTER 9

## Future Facing

### Heading into Our Mission

---

*The future belongs to those who believe
in the beauty of their dreams.*
**—ELEANOR ROOSEVELT**

---

Our company has a legacy of fifty years—and now we are driving toward our future. The essence of our philosophy as a property management company is rooted in building lasting relationships and enhancing value with every decision we make. Now I'm responsible for shaping the vision for the *next* fifty years, which means future-proofing our company while keeping the owner mindset that has always defined us.

In terms of property management excellence, future-proofing a management company involves implementing strategies that ensure the business remains resilient, adaptable, agile, and competitive in the face of evolving industry trends, technological advancements, and changing market conditions. Here are several key strategies for ensuring property management excellence in the future—actionable tips you can apply to your business.

# Embrace Technology and Automation

As I shared earlier in the book, sometimes our company has acquired a property, or has been hired to manage it, only to discover the processes in place were more suited to the 1980s—even paper tenant files in old green-metal file cabinets. I try to leverage as much technology and automation and efficiency as possible. However—and this is so important—*relationships* are what drives value in the way we do things. Automation and efficiencies should not lose the human touch—they should enhance it and make us *more* responsive and attuned to our clients' and tenants' needs.

Implementing advanced property management software can streamline operations, improve efficiency, and enhance tenant and client experiences. Features such as online rent payments, maintenance request tracking, and lease management automation reduce administrative burdens and improve service delivery—meaning you as a property manager can focus on other things. It means our people in the field can concentrate on their most important tasks.

Our industry, and every industry, is also starting to utilize data and analytics to gain insights into market trends, tenant behaviors, and property performance. Data-driven decision-making helps optimize rental rates, improve tenant retention, and identify areas for operational improvement.

Therefore, keep in mind, if you are a property manager, you have collected extensive client and tenant data—from credit checks, to past addresses, to Social Security numbers, and personal references. With the increasing reliance on digital systems, property management companies must protect tenant and client data from cyberattacks. This involves implementing robust cybersecurity measures, such as encryption, regular security audits, and staff training.

We have seen over and over the public hit that such data breaches bring to a company's reputation. It erodes public trust—and the trust of tenants, clients, and investors. In addition, an outage of critical software systems could disrupt operations, from rent collection to maintenance requests. Property managers should have backup systems and a disaster recovery plan to minimize downtime.

Technology and automation also include smart building technologies. Incorporating smart Internet of Things (IoT) devices for energy management, security systems, and remote monitoring can enhance property value, reduce operational costs, and attract tech-savvy tenants. Other technology can include 5G, smart lighting (reduced electricity costs by turning off lights when no one is present), and other management systems.

Automation can also improve sustainability through efficiencies. Embrace sustainability by incorporating energy-efficient appliances, water-saving fixtures, and renewable energy sources into properties. Green building practices not only reduce operating costs but also appeal to environmentally conscious tenants and investors. Leadership in Energy and Environmental Design (LEED) or Energy Star certifications for your properties also show a commitment to sustainable practices. These certifications can enhance property value, enhance your reputation, and attract quality tenants—especially in commercial properties.

Proptech is rapidly changing the real estate and property management industries. While some of these innovations are not widespread yet (such as blockchain for property transactions), we have seen how fast tech changes our lives. Adopting relevant technologies can streamline operations and give your company a competitive edge.

Here are the key technology investments and sustainability initiatives to consider implementing in your property management business:

## TECHNOLOGY INVESTMENTS

**Property management software**: Online rent payments, maintenance request tracking, and lease management automation.

**Data analytics platforms**: For optimizing rental pricing, improving tenant retention, and tracking property performance.

**Cybersecurity solutions**: Encryption, regular security audits, and staff training on data protection.

**Backup systems and disaster recovery plans**: Ensure continuity during power outages or software system failures.

**Smart building technologies**: Incorporate IoT devices for energy management, security systems, and remote monitoring.

**5G connectivity**: For enhanced internet performance in residential and commercial properties.

**Smart lighting systems**: Automatically turn off lights when rooms are unoccupied to save energy.

CHAPTER 9

# Future-Proofing with Diversification—or Niches

To future-proof your property management business, diversification can be a game changer. Expanding beyond traditional property management services allows you to create new revenue streams and attract a broader client base. Whether you're diversifying your portfolio or offering complementary services, this approach ensures that your business remains resilient in an ever-changing market.

Consider offering additional services such as facility management, real estate consulting, or short-term rental management. Each of these can open up opportunities to serve different types of clients, adding stability and flexibility to your business. For example, real estate consulting could appeal to investors looking for expert advice, while short-term rental management can help you tap into the lucrative vacation rental market.

Alternatively, focusing on a niche market can set your company apart from competitors. By specializing in specific sectors, you can carve out a space in high-demand markets. Some niches to consider include:

- **Luxury properties:** Catering to high-end residential or commercial properties often brings higher rental rates, along with clientele willing to pay for premium services.

- **Senior housing:** With an aging population, senior living facilities are in increasing demand, and this market is considered recession resistant.

- **Student housing:** College towns have a steady demand for student housing, providing consistent returns even during economic downturns.

J. P. Morgan has noted that sectors like senior housing and student housing are particularly resilient in tough economic times. Specializing in these areas not only helps differentiate your company but also ensures your business is less vulnerable to market fluctuations.

In addition to targeting niche markets, offering value-added services can further enhance your business, such as the following:

- Property maintenance and repairs
- Landscaping and groundskeeping
- Cleaning and janitorial services
- Concierge or lifestyle services for luxury properties

These services not only generate additional income but also improve the tenant experience, leading to higher tenant retention and lower vacancy rates. Tenants who feel well cared for are more likely to stay longer, which ultimately benefits your bottom line.

# Invest in Staff Development and Training

Investing in our team members' development and training is very important to Lauren and me. You might recall that she initially came aboard in a human resources capacity. As an empathic person and a trained social worker, she is the type of person who wants to get to know our staff and learn what makes them tick.

One of the "surprises" Lauren discovered is that yes, we must pay people fairly, and yes, it is nice when your supervisor or the company owner brings in chocolates or donuts. But when we *asked* our people what they really wanted—especially in the midst of the pandemic—the overwhelming responses were growth, development, and training.

Thus, we encourage ongoing professional development for our staff by providing access to industry certifications, workshops, and training programs. When someone completes a program, they are reimbursed at 100 percent—even if they want to invest the time to go through all the coursework to become a real estate salesperson. If they can gain knowledge and skills for property management, we are all for it.

We aim to create a positive work environment that values employee contributions, offers competitive compensation, and provides opportunities for career growth. Retaining top talent is crucial for maintaining a high level of service and ensuring long-term success. I also want to remind readers that "top talent" does not necessarily mean the person with the most experience. We love training people we can see have a fire inside for the fast-paced world of property management—and love to develop them, teaching them our values and way of doing things.

**Property Management Excellence Tip:**

Here are five ways to invest in your team:
1. Offer industry certifications and reimburse education costs
2. Create a culture of continuous learning
3. Recognize potential, not just experience
4. Provide career growth opportunities
5. Listen to your team's needs

# Future-Proofing by Having Crisis Plans

No one saw COVID-19 coming. I was actually lucky, in a way, that I was alerted to a virus in Asia by a client of mine. I immediately began formulating our plan. When the pandemic really hit the States and everything shut down, we were ready.

I hope we never see another pandemic—but the reality is that we will likely experience another emergency of a similar magnitude, even if it's not a global pandemic again. Whether those are natural disasters or climate-related crises or other "worst cases" that a property manager needs to prepare for in order to future-proof both their portfolio and the safety of their tenants, employees, and operations.

> **WORST-CASE SCENARIOS TO PREPARE FOR**
>
> - Natural disasters, including floods, wildfires, earthquakes, tornados, and hurricanes.
> - Snow and ice and other, more common, weather occurrences (including, these days, extreme heat) need to be planned for, including snow and ice removal procedures, HVAC and water supply contingency plans, and checks on vulnerable tenants.
> - Building fires can occur at any time, and property managers must ensure that fire alarms and sprinkler systems are regularly tested, fire extinguishers are accessible, and evacuation routes are clearly marked and communicated to tenants.
> - Pandemics and infectious outbreaks: Before the COVID-19 pandemic, I don't know that I had ever thought about what would happen if no one could leave their house (California

# CHAPTER 9

> was especially strict with their lockdown procedures), or if people needed to wear masks and stay six feet apart in common areas in our buildings. The COVID-19 pandemic highlighted the need for comprehensive plans to handle infectious disease outbreaks. Property managers should be prepared to implement social distancing measures, enhanced cleaning protocols, and communication plans to keep tenants informed of health guidelines.
> - Power outages and water supply interruptions can severely disrupt tenants' lives and work. Power failures can disrupt building operations, particularly in multiunit properties with elevators, security systems, and electronic access controls. Backup generators, battery-operated emergency lights, and manual override options should be part of any preparedness plan. Water supply issues can stem from main breaks, droughts, or contamination.
> - Security threats, active shooters, domestic violence incidents, burglaries, and other situations can disrupt the security measures your properties may have in effect. There should be crisis plans for such potential events.

Plan for the worst—and hopefully it will never come to pass.

## Future-Proofing Your Financial Picture

When the COVID-19 crisis first emerged, George and I immediately got to work reaching out to tenants and landlords, investors, and our team to begin developing potential financial plans for this unprecedented situation. I saw firsthand that future-proofing includes planning for economic downturns, such as building reserves, being financially able to offer flexible payment plans to tenants, and diversifying our real estate portfolio.

I will say the experience strengthened our client relationships and reputation—because we were seen as building trust and creating understanding. Our policies of transparency and clear communication with property owners and investors are crucial for future proofing. Provide regular, detailed reports on property performance, financials, and market conditions to keep clients informed and confident in your management.

# Future-Proof Your Brand

Establish your company as a leader in the industry by consistently delivering high-quality services and maintaining a strong online presence. Encourage satisfied clients and tenants to leave positive reviews and address any negative feedback promptly and professionally.

I will add that, again, online is wonderful—but training your people to develop relationships needs to be an equal part of the equation.

I try to participate in industry associations, attend conferences, and engage with other professionals in the real estate and property management sectors. Real estate is a team sport and a space of abundance. Networking can lead to new business opportunities, partnerships, and valuable insights. I also sit on nonprofit boards—and add my voice to committees on homelessness, affordable housing, and development plans. No one can future-proof their business by being siloed. Getting out there in entrepreneurial organizations, in community organizations that resonate with you, can help you see your business reach the next milestone.

CHAPTER 9

# Future-Proof by Being Willing to Change

One of the key lessons in future-proofing is learning to embrace change, even when it's uncomfortable. Lauren, who has a natural gift for training, helped us navigate this very challenge. I still remember when we had a massive, shared work document that caused constant headaches—crashing everyone's computers and making collaboration impossible. It was clear that the system wasn't working, but like many companies, we had been using it because that's just how things had always been done.

Lauren saw the inefficiency immediately and took action. She didn't just find a better platform to manage our standard operating procedures (SOPs)—she built a whole new system from the ground up, creating a user-friendly platform with our software partner, Whale, that the entire team could access and utilize seamlessly.

But Lauren didn't stop there. True to her nature, she went beyond simply implementing a solution; she developed training modules and quizzes to ensure that everyone fully understood how to use the new system. This approach not only improved operational efficiency but also ensured that our staff was properly trained and confident in using the new technology.

Now we're taking things a step further. Lauren and I are partnering with the same technology company that helped us build the platform, and we're working to create a comprehensive community for training property managers and real estate investors. This next phase ties back to our core belief: leverage technology in ways that enhance both operations and people's growth.

The real lesson here is that future-proofing requires identifying inefficiencies and being bold enough to change them, even when it's tough. Leaders often have to face transformational tasks head-on, and yes, they're hard—really hard. But it's those tough changes that will ultimately future-proof your company and ensure long-term success.

And to be transparent, future-proofing Coastline Equity has meant I've had to change too. I have a tendency to move too fast (the "ADHD superpower" that sometimes backfires). I'm constantly pushing for faster results, often expecting that if I have an idea today, it should be completed yesterday.

That's where Lauren comes in. She challenges me, reminding me to slow down and give our team the time they need to truly absorb and implement changes. Her background in social work and training has taught me there's a better way to lead and train—one that focuses on pacing, training, and making sure our people are set up for success.

## Develop a Long-Term Vision

As I prepared to take the reins after George retired, I was energized by the opportunity to shape the company's long-term, future-facing vision. We would continue to do the great things the company had always done, but I had ambitious goals that I not only developed for myself—but that I wanted to share with our people.

I remember when I announced that Lauren and I would be giving 50 percent of our profits to philanthropic endeavors. I think the room took a collective breath. But we also said we would match the giving of our employees and the causes that mattered to them. Not only was that important from the perspective of demonstrating our community commitment, but it also said to our team that we wanted them to be part of our long-term vision too.

I have a habit where I walk my dog in the morning, often taking a notebook and pen and sitting by the water to journal, write business articles, and just *think*. It is important to develop a long-term strategic plan (and a method to get it out of your head) that outlines your company's vision, goals, and growth strategies. Regularly review and update this plan to reflect changes in the market, industry trends, and company performance. I sit by the water, journal, and let my thoughts wander—focusing on what the future holds for our company.

This routine has taught me the importance of crafting a long-term strategic plan—one that outlines your company's vision, goals, and strategies for growth. But a plan isn't static. It requires regular review and updates to account for shifts in the market, industry trends, and company performance. Flexibility is key; your vision needs to evolve as your business and the world around you do.

Part of the long-term vision is to prepare for leadership transitions by developing a succession plan that identifies potential future leaders within the company. Ensuring a smooth leadership transition is critical for maintaining continuity and achieving long-term success. George worked into his eighties! I don't know what is in store for me, but I do know the vision for our company is bigger than just me.

# Key Elements of a Strong Strategic Vision

Here are some key elements that I believe help create the best strategic vision as a business leader:

- **Purpose-driven goals:** A strong vision is rooted in purpose, the "why." Align your long-term strategy with goals that go beyond profit, focusing on how your business can positively impact your team, clients, and the community.

- **Adaptability:** A strategic vision needs to be flexible. Markets, industries, and technologies evolve—your vision must evolve with them. Build adaptability into your plan so that you can pivot as needed.

- **Team alignment:** A vision is only powerful if your entire team is on board. Engage your employees in the development of your vision and ensure they understand how their contributions fit into the larger goals.

- **Data-driven decisions:** Use data and analytics to inform your long-term strategy. A strategic vision that combines big-picture goals with real-time market insights is more likely to succeed.

- **Succession planning:** A sustainable vision must account for future leadership transitions. Develop potential future leaders within the company to ensure continuity and maintain company culture.

- **Community impact:** Incorporate a plan for how your business will give back to the community. This could involve philanthropy, local initiatives, or sustainability practices that make a lasting positive difference.

- **Long-term financial planning:** Ensure that your strategic vision includes a strong financial foundation, with plans for building reserves, managing cash flow, and diversifying income streams to weather economic fluctuations.

- **Transparency and communication:** Clearly communicate your vision to stakeholders—whether it's your employees, investors, or clients. Transparency builds trust and alignment, ensuring that everyone works toward the same goals.

\*\*\*

# CHAPTER 9

Future-proofing a property management company requires a proactive approach to embracing technology, focusing on sustainability, enhancing tenant and client relationships, and staying adaptable to industry changes. By investing in staff development, diversifying revenue streams, and adopting innovative solutions, property managers can ensure their business remains resilient and competitive in the years to come. With a clear long-term vision and a commitment to excellence, property management companies can navigate the challenges of the future and continue to thrive in an evolving landscape.

# CONCLUSION

## Full Circle

When we began this book, I talked about the 110 Freeway—where it seems to end, right at the edge of San Pedro. For many growing up in neighborhoods like mine, it felt like life came to a dead end too. But what I've learned is that endings are often just new beginnings in disguise. I never could have imagined that the kid who sought refuge at the Boys & Girls Club would eventually find his path to the future by reconnecting with his past.

Just like the 110's apparent dead end, I came to realize that what seemed like barriers were actually opportunities. The challenges I faced growing up in Section 8 housing became the foundation for my passion for housing and property management. I saw how much a stable home—or the lack of one—can impact a family's sense of security, hope, and future. Those early experiences ignited a drive in me to help create quality housing, and as I stepped into this field, I quickly understood that my background, which should have set me up for failure, became my superpower. It gave me the ability to see the potential in properties—and more importantly, in people.

## PROPERTY MANAGEMENT EXCELLENCE

Property management is complicated. It's not a simple nine-to-five job, and if you're looking for predictability, this career might not be for you. But if you love the challenge of turning problems into solutions, of navigating crises and finding new opportunities in the midst of them, then you might just thrive in this industry. Despite the complexity of my career and the pressures of leading a company, the lessons of leadership I learned back at that Boys & Girls Club remain simple:

> 1. **Treat all people with dignity.**
> 2. **Speak up for those less fortunate.**
> 3. **Give people a chance—see their potential.**
> 4. **Pay it forward.**
> 5. **Turn adversity into your strength.**
> 6. **Do the right thing.**

I could never have predicted the twists and turns my career would take, but each one has brought me to this moment. From becoming a CEO in my midthirties to developing a vision of philanthropy alongside Lauren, to traveling to places I once only dreamed about—it's been a journey beyond what I could have imagined as a kid from my neighborhood. Yet every step along the way, I've applied the same principles I learned as a child at the Boys & Girls Club to the world of real estate.

I wrote this book not just to share my story but also to offer the lessons I've learned to others—whether you're an investor, a property manager, someone considering a career in this industry, an entrepreneur, or a community member who wants to better understand the impact of real estate on people's lives. Coastline Equity is redefining excellence in property management. We've built a reputation based on trust, driven by a diverse portfolio that reflects both timeless principles and modern strategies. Our success comes from blending cutting-edge technology with old-school relationship building—staying true to the values that got us here, while embracing the future.

And speaking of the future—just as the 110 Freeway seems to end in San Pedro, I came to realize that was far from the truth. My journey in property management is really just beginning. What once felt like a dead end has become the foundation for something far greater. Now, instead of feeling trapped at the end of a road, I'm building new highways of opportunity for our team, our clients, and our community.

Thank you for taking this journey with me. I hope this book has shown you that investing in real estate and building a real estate portfolio can be a smart way to secure your financial future. But more than that, I hope it has given you insight into how this industry can work—not just for profit, but for people. My dream is for property management CEOs to come together and set new standards that protect everyone involved, from investors to tenants, from managers to communities.

Finally, this is a heartfelt thank-you to our clients for the faith they've placed in us, and to our incredible team. When I think about the ambitious plans we have for Coastline Equity's future, I know that excellence is at the core of everything we do. It's been quite a journey so far, and I can't wait to see where the next highway takes us.

# ABOUT THE AUTHOR

Anthony A. Luna is a respected leader in the property management industry, known for his innovative approach, commitment to community building, and passion for delivering exceptional results. Anthony's life story is a testament to the transformative power of mentorship, resilience, and finding one's calling in service to others. His experience has instilled in him a deep understanding of the importance of quality living and working environments, which he integrates into his business practices.

As chief executive officer of Coastline Equity, Anthony oversees property management, asset management, and real estate investment services. He has successfully managed a diverse portfolio of properties, consistently exceeding client expectations by significantly increasing property value and profitability.

Under Anthony's leadership, Coastline Equity has set new industry standards for social responsibility and ethical business practices. His approach goes beyond profit, creating lasting impacts in the communities they serve. He shares the lessons he has learned from making a difference in the real estate industry as a frequent contributor to *Forbes*, FastCompany, and other prominent publications.

Beyond his professional achievements, Anthony is a dedicated advocate for economic development and community support. He has served on the Leadership Council of the National Small Business Association, where he championed policies to benefit small businesses nationwide. Locally, he has been a board member of the San Pedro Chamber of Commerce, focusing on initiatives to foster a thriving local economy. Anthony now serves on the board of the Boys & Girls Clubs of the Los Angeles Harbor—the very Club that once believed in him, and which he credits with saving his life and making his journey to Property Management Excellence possible. It was there he first experienced the power of mentors who made him—and thousands of other young people—feel seen, supported, and empowered to rise.

Today, he gives back not just as a leader, but as living proof of the Club's mission in action.

# CONNECT WITH ANTHONY A. LUNA

Anthony A. Luna lives in San Pedro, California, and is pleased to connect with his readers professionally and socially.

To connect with Anthony and learn more about Coastline Equity's values-based approach to property management, please scan the QR code above.